Contents

EDITOR'S NOTES

Leadership is about change. In times of rapid change, effective leaders must be able not only to cope with the environment but also to shape it. Simply put, "leaders are agents of change—persons whose acts affect other people more than other people's acts affect them" (Bass, 1990, pp. 19–20).

The context, then, is continuous change. Contemporary community college leaders must develop adaptive skills and competencies commensurate with expanding missions and challenging fiscal alternatives. Peter Drucker (1999) recognized that one cannot *manage* change; one can only be ahead of it. This volume provides new ways of looking at change leadership, at the competencies required to be a change leader, and at the programs aimed at developing effective leaders.

Community expectations of college leaders have never been higher. Although community college leaders have always taken great pride in being responsive to their communities, and must continue to do so, institutions are no longer limited to narrow geographic boundaries. Protectionism and parochialism are out; partnerships and collaboration are in. Issues of access, alternative pathways from the high school and to the university, an increasing number of students whose first language is not English, all this coupled with dwindling resources requires creative thinking and problem-solving skills. Societal needs and emerging challenges call for new strategies and experiences in leadership preparation (Davis, 2003; Fullan, 2001; Heifetz and Laurie, 1998; Kouzes and Posner, 2002).

Piland and Wolf (2003) recognized the fact that "community college leadership has never been more complex and challenging" (p. 1). They also bemoaned "the typically poor sets of support systems and local institutional incentives and policies that would encourage leadership development" (p. 1).

This volume of *New Directions for Community Colleges* builds on the work of Piland and Wolf and focuses on leadership development at all levels; the importance of vision and foresight; the relevance of partnerships; and best practices in a rapidly changing economic, social, political, and cultural environment. The chapter authors bring unique perspectives through their strength as recognized scholars in leadership studies as well as practitioners who are actively engaged in leadership in community colleges. Both empirical studies and best practices are included to further knowledge and understanding of effective leadership in the context of change.

Chapter One reviews the historical and theoretical underpinnings of change and change leadership, particularly as it applies to community colleges. Chapter Two discusses change leadership and its role in effective

partnerships, while Chapter Three looks at creation of dynamic teams as part of leadership development. Chapters Four, Five, and Six introduce three model leadership development programs, with emphasis on the new types of change leaders needed in today's colleges. Two are university-based programs and the third is an AACC Council–based program. Chapter Seven discusses the many types of leadership programs available to middle managers aspiring to become more effective leaders of change in their institution. Chapter Eight looks at the challenges presidents face when confronted with a crisis and suggests the resultant opportunity to grow as a change leader. Finally, Chapter Nine reviews the nature of leadership and brings together the major issues and challenges in leadership development in the context of change.

Desna Wallin leads off the volume with a discussion of change leadership and its relevance to contemporary community colleges. A review of the context of change suggests that change leadership differs in important ways from leadership that may be effective during times of relative stability. Thus, organizers responsible for designing and developing leadership programs should pay particular attention to those competencies and skills that are important for today's change leaders.

Marilyn Amey discusses the characteristics of effective partnerships, with emphasis on the qualities of leadership necessary to sustain such partnerships. She notes that partnerships are complex and labor intensive and require flexibility and adaptability. However, such partnerships may be effective strategies to achieve organizational goals, particularly if resources are tight and learner needs are increasing.

Matthew Basham and Raghu Mathur examine the use of teams and the role of team leaders. Using the research of several Harvard scholars as a framework, the authors call on Kotter's distinction between leaders and managers emphasizing that both are needed in successful teams. Ongoing or static teams, they maintain, run the risk of becoming stale, while dynamic teams may serve the institution through more effective use of the skills and talents of both managers and leaders.

Dale Campbell, Syraj Syed, and Phillip A. Morris present the University of Florida's leadership development program, emphasizing understanding of leadership attributes and the work styles of successful leaders. They discuss the gap in traditional leadership programs and describe ways to implement targeted improvements in essential interpersonal competencies for change leaders.

Leila Gonzalez Sullivan and Colleen Aalsburg Wiessner highlight the innovative leadership program developed by the National Community College Hispanic Council, an affiliate of the American Association of Community Colleges. Specifically, they discuss the outcomes related to including a reflection component in the program.

Janice Nahra Friedel discusses major factors considered in starting a new EdD program in community college leadership at California State University Northridge. The program is seen as an opportunity to make the doctorate unique, balancing the needs of students as well as faculty change leaders with the realities of budgetary limitations.

Larry Ebbers, Kitty Conover, and Anisha Samuels take the big-picture view in looking at a number of leadership development programs. From "grow your own" to state, regional, and national programs, all have something to offer, particularly for the midlevel manager wanting to advance a career.

Deborah Floyd, Pat Maslin-Ostrowski, and Michael Hrabak take an unusual approach to presidential leadership development in a crisis or "wounding" situation. Crises and dilemmas are inevitable components of leadership. Inasmuch as the leader inhabits the realm of action and is a change agent, he or she is engaged in risky work. The authors emphasize the importance of strong support systems and offer practical recommendations to equip aspiring and practicing community college presidents.

In the final chapter Robert Cloud offers an overview and history of leadership and places this work within that history. It is hoped that this volume, with its mix of theoretical and applied approaches to change leadership, contributes meaningfully to the limited existing literature regarding change leadership in community colleges. Contemporary community college leaders will require increasingly sophisticated preparation to develop the skills and understandings needed to successfully negotiate and lead in a context of change.

Desna L. Wallin
Editor

References

Bass, B. M. *Bass & Stogdill's Handbook of Leadership*. New York: Free Press, 1990.

Davis, J. R. *Learning to Lead*. Westport, Conn.: Praeger, 2003.

Drucker, P. F. *Management Challenges for the 21st Century*. New York: HarperCollins, 1999.

Fullan, M. *Leading in a Culture of Change*. San Francisco: Jossey-Bass, 2001.

Heifetz, R. A., and Laurie, D. L. "The Work of Leadership." In *Harvard Business Review on Leadership*. Boston, Mass.: Harvard Business School, 1998, 171–198.

Kouzes, J. M, and Posner, B. Z. *The Leadership Challenge*. San Francisco: Jossey-Bass, 2002.

Piland, W. E., and Wolf, D. B. (eds.). *Help Wanted: Preparing Community College Leaders in a New Century*. In New Directions for Community Colleges, no. 123. San Francisco: Jossey-Bass, 2003.

DESNA L. WALLIN *is associate professor in the Department of Lifelong Education, Administration, and Policy at the University of Georgia. She has also served as president of Clinton Community College in Iowa and Forsyth Technical Community College in North Carolina.*

1

*Creating a culture of change is a challenge to any leader.
Change leadership in tomorrow's successful colleges will
foster leaders who can anticipate change, analyze the
environment, act decisively and collaboratively, and
affirm the value of positive change.*

Looking to the Future: Change Leaders for Tomorrow's Community Colleges

Desna L. Wallin

The old ways of managing and organizing and leading are no longer effective. The current environment calls for a different set of leadership skills from those that might have sufficed in less turbulent times. Earlier ways of predicting, modeling, and planning do not serve as well as they once did. The rational theories of management and bureaucratic order developed by Frederick Taylor and Max Weber no longer seem to be applicable (Mintzberg, 1998; Wallin and Ryan, 1994). Cohen and March (1986) point out that "leadership seems to be less a matter of straightforward instrumental action and hierarchical control than is anticipated by classical descriptions" (p. xiv).

Community colleges are changing as well, and the roles of community college leaders at all levels are in flux. Cohen and March (1986) anticipated change leadership when they suggested that in a world so difficult to predict and control, an approach recognizing ambiguity is both appropriate and useful. In fact, they posit that colleges can be seen as "changing continuously in response to various internal and external pressures and opportunities" (p. xvi). Bureaucratic practices built up over the years now stand as barriers. The role of the change leader is to remove barriers and free people to use their strengths to improve the organization, make it responsive to the community and to regional and national needs, and to look with fresh vision on the landscape that has become the field of labor for community colleges. Although it is apparent that the old models do not work as well as they once did, research and models for effective change leadership in contemporary community colleges seem to be lacking in the current literature.

NEW DIRECTIONS FOR COMMUNITY COLLEGES, no. 149, Spring 2010 © 2010 Wiley Periodicals, Inc.
Published online in Wiley InterScience (www.interscience.wiley.com) • DOI: 10.1002/cc.390

This volume anticipates contributing to the existing body of literature regarding change leadership.

Contemporary change leaders must look critically at their organization and the environment in which it functions. Further, they need to effectively manage themselves (Bennis, 1989; Bennis and Nanus, 1985; Drucker, 1999) as leaders. Change leaders need to be "EQ smart" (Cooper and Sawaf, 1997)—perceptive, intuitive, and reflective—as well as IQ smart to be effective. In fact, Bennis suggests that "leadership is first being then doing. Everything the leader does reflects what he or she is" (1989, p. 141). Wheatley (1999) adds to the importance of the leader's self-awareness when she maintains that leaders are "obligated to help the whole orga-nization look at itself, to be reflective and learningful about its activities and decisions" (p. 131). Change leaders build inclusive learning commu-nities and seek out new leaders to encourage and mentor. In fact, "institu-tionalizing a leadership-centered culture is the ultimate act of leadership" (Kotter, 1998, p. 53). This is the new reality for change leaders.

Leadership is a multifaceted concept; there are as many definitions of leadership as there are scholars of the subject. In a review of prior studies, Northouse (2007) suggests that in the past sixty years there have been as many as sixty-five classification systems proposed to explain the dimensions of leadership. For the purpose of change leadership, however, a few defini-tions are particularly important. Bennis (1989) maintains that before any-one can learn to lead, he or she "must learn something about this strange new world. Indeed, anyone who does not master this mercurial content will be mastered by it" (p. 2). De Pree (1989) concurs with his view that "lead-ership is an art, something to be learned over time, not simply by reading books. Leadership is more tribal than scientific, more a weaving of relation-ships than an amassing of information" (p. 3). Northouse (2007) sees lead-ership as "a process whereby an individual influences a group of individuals to achieve a common goal" (p. 3). It includes influence, it involves groups, and it demands attention to goals. Fullan (2001) sees change leadership through the lens of complexity: "The more complex society gets, the more sophisticated leadership must become. Complexity means change, but specifically it means rapidly occurring, unpredictable, nonlinear change" (p. ix). This characteristic of nonlinear change means that even though organizations change in response to their environment, "they rarely change in a way that fulfills the intentional plan of a single group of actors" (Cohen and March, 1986, p. 275). Beach (2006) looks at leadership as "the art of producing appropriate changes in an organization's external environment, its functions and structure, its culture, and its practices in pursuit of sur-vival and prosperity" (p. ix). In other words, he sees change as an integral part of leadership. Finally, harking back in history for a meaningful defini-tion of contemporary change leadership, we may recall that Winston Churchill once defined leadership as "going from failure to failure without losing enthusiasm" (Senge, Scharmer, Jaworski, and Flowers, 2004, p. 149)—a way of looking at leadership that might be particularly meaningful to current change leaders!

Change leadership exemplifies many of the attributes of the better-known transformational leadership. Transformational leadership is a process that changes and transforms followers: "It is concerned with emotions, values, ethics, standards, and long-term goals and includes assessing followers' motives, satisfying their needs, and treating them as full human beings. Transformational leadership involves an exceptional form of influence that moves followers to accomplish more than what is usually expected of them" (Northouse, 2007, pp. 175–176). It was the work of Burns, however, that "laid the foundation for the concept of transformational leaders, who can create a vision for change, communicate it to others, and then help those others to accomplish that vision through their own commitment to it. Thus, while transactional leaders manage and maintain, transformational leaders promote fundamental change in the organization, helping the organization adjust to the varying needs of today's rapidly changing society" (Roueche, Baker, and Rose, 1989, p. 35). The emphasis in transformational leadership is on a process that changes and transforms individuals. Transformational leaders frequently act as change agents in their organizations, but changes in the organization are of secondary concern relative to changes in individuals.

Change leadership, however, even though embodying transformational leadership, is both broader and deeper, involving individual and organizational change alike. Its theoretical roots emanate from Lewin's three steps of organizational change: unfreeze, change, and refreeze. Unfreezing is related to creating willingness and motivation for change through anticipating the future and analyzing the possibilities of change, change means seeing things differently and acting to move toward a more desired state, and refreezing establishes new ways to affirm the change and secure the new desired behavior (Burke, 2008). Change leadership at its core involves an ongoing search for better ways of doing things. Change leaders are constantly identifying potential opportunities and threats; they are aware of and anticipate changes in the environment that might affect the college and its mission. Change leadership is a process that anticipates change; requires analysis of the internal and external environment; acts by means of appropriate and timely data and the strengths of team members; and is reflective in affirming, sustaining, and reviewing actions with a mind-set of continuous organizational improvement.

Four Essential Characteristics of Change Leadership

In fact, change leadership can be seen to embody four essential characteristics, what might be called the four A's of change leadership. First, change leadership *anticipates*. It is visionary and forward-looking. It avoids reactionary thinking and acting. Second, change leadership is constantly *analyzing* the environment, both internal and external, to gather reliable data on which to make decisions. It engages in strategic and tactical planning to make the most of the moment. Third, change leadership *acts*. With a vision and a plan, with accurate and current data, action is collaborative and inclusive; however, it is also immediate and decisive. It builds on the strengths of team members. It is accountable to stakeholders. Finally, change leadership *affirms*. It is not enough to have a vision, a plan, and action. Once action is implemented, attention is given to continuing to review and affirm the change. Here is a summary of these four characteristics of change leadership.

Anticipate. Drucker (1999) was very much aware of the importance of anticipating change in organizations. He claimed that "one cannot manage change. One can only be ahead of it" (p. 73). Community college leaders operate in an environment of volatility, which requires them to be ahead of change. Tichy and DeVanna (1990) studied how leaders anticipate change. They wanted to understand how leaders anticipate change in conditions of rapid technological changes, social and cultural changes, and increased competition, all of which apply to today's community colleges. Their findings suggested a three-act process for anticipating change: (1) recognizing the need for change, (2) creating a vision for that change, and (3) institutionalizing change.

Analyze. Bennis (1989) rightly observes that "resisting change is as futile as resisting weather, and change is our weather now. It is that constant and that unpredictable. Leaders live in it, and so do organizations. And there is much organizations can do to make the process easier" (p. 172). One thing a change leader must do to act as a catalyst for change in an organization is carefully analyze, examine, and understand the environment, both internal and external, in which the college works. This includes gathering accurate and timely information to base one's actions on. It also includes strategic and tactical planning. Beach (2006) suggests that even though leadership is about change, it is not about arbitrary change. Change for the sake of change is most often detrimental and destabilizing to an organization. He maintains that a continuous assessing of the environment is critically important to initiating successful change efforts. Assessing the environment, internal and external, is one of the primary responsibilities of a change leader: "The leader's job is to make the organization a viable participant in the game by fostering an understanding of its external and internal environments and by promoting changes in both of them that enhance its ability to react to or anticipate opportunities and threats, with the goal of surviving and prospering" (2006, p. 2).

Act. The art of leadership, according to De Pree (1989), is "liberating people to do what is required of them in the most effective and humane way possible" (p. xx). It is preparing them to act, both individually and as members of a team. Building on the existing strengths of teams is the key to successful organizational change. The Gallup organization's leadership assessment, *StrengthsFinder* (Rath, 2007), the result of an extensive longitudinal study, found that organizations spend far more time and money on trying to buttress employee weaknesses than they do building on existing strengths and talents. Their studies show that "people who do have the opportunity to focus on their strengths every day are six times as likely to be engaged in their jobs and more than three times as likely to report having an excellent quality of life in general" (p. iii). If a college is to be accountable, and to act quickly with insight and integrity, it must expend resources in developing and growing its internal leadership at all levels, not just at the top. Riggs (2009) emphasizes the importance of midlevel leadership. Presidential leadership is critical, but it is the midlevel leaders, the deans, vice presidents, directors, and others who carry out many of the functions of the college and are responsible for much of the success of the college.

Affirm. "Transformation begins with trust. Trust is the essential link between leader and led, vital to people's job satisfaction and loyalty, vital to followership. It is doubly important when organizations are seeking rapid improvement, which requires exceptional effort and competence" (Evans, 2000, p. 287). Leaders need to be able to instill trust in followers if they hope to sustain meaningful change. Implementation of change is never simple and rarely linear. Unexpected problems and unanticipated issues will develop; there is no doubt that it is difficult to maintain change. Wheatley (1999) summarized the challenge of maintaining change when she observed that "any living thing will change only if it sees change as the means of preserving itself" (p. 147). So it is important for the change leader to realize that many organizational changes translate to personal or professional loss for individuals. It is vital for the change leader to be reflective, constantly review and reassess changes, and communicate openly and frequently about them. As O'Banion has suggested (2008), in many ways it is not as much fun to work in community colleges as it once was: "Being a leader in today's environment and dealing with enormous change are challenges that require special skills and abilities, patience, humor, and courage that exceed by far that required of leaders 40 years ago" (p. 1). Being reflective and affirming in implementing and sustaining change is one of those special skills and abilities required of today's change leaders.

Conclusion

Lorenzo and DeMarte (2002) make the point that there is nothing particularly new about the call for organizational change and for leaders to take the helm as champions of change. They maintain that

> there is almost unanimous accord that tomorrow's leaders must become adept at reshaping their organizations in fundamental ways. These strong and

pervasive sentiments lead to two basic assumptions about the future of community colleges. First, to remain viable, community colleges must continue to change in significant ways. Second, the colleges' success will probably be determined by their ability to recruit and develop effective leaders [p. 47].

Perhaps what is new is an increasing interest on the part of graduate programs, grow-your-own local leadership programs, and professional association leadership programs in the concept of change leadership. Perhaps it is the realization that things really are changing, that tomorrow will not be the same as yesterday, regardless of the politics or the economy of the nation. Drucker (1999) insists that change leaders must abandon yesterday if they are to act on today:

> The first need is to free resources from being committed to maintaining what no longer contributes to performance, and no longer produces results. . . . To maintain yesterday is always difficult and extremely time-consuming. To maintain yesterday therefore always commits the institution's scarcest and most valuable resources—and above all its ablest people—to nonresults [p. 74].

Thus, if a college believes the future lies in training students for green jobs, something currently within the curriculum has to be deleted. Resources—dollars and personnel—cannot be extended to cover both existing and declining programs while funding and staffing new and innovative programs; "it is futile . . . to ignore the changes and to pretend that tomorrow will be like yesterday, only more so" (Drucker, 1999, p. 92). This is the type of policy and practice most likely to be adopted by institutions that were successful in earlier periods. Those organizations are likely to suffer from the delusion that tomorrow will be like yesterday. Community colleges have been remarkably successful in the past; that is no guarantee they will continue to be. Community colleges and their leaders must be vigilant to ensure that the institutions have both the resources and the leadership to make necessary changes to remain successful.

The chapters that follow in this volume are illustrative of change leadership in a variety of settings and circumstances. Amey discusses the abilities of change leaders to understand and implement mutually beneficial partnerships, while Basham and Mathur look at the role of teams in rapidly changing environments. Three chapters deal with the emerging research and practice in preparing change leaders. Campbell and colleagues examine a leadership program that emphasizes assessment to develop change leaders; Sullivan and Wiessner review a program targeting Hispanic leaders that highlights the importance of reflection for change leaders; and Friedel describes the components and development of a new doctoral program focused on preparing leaders to act as change agents. Ebbers and coauthors detail the importance of leadership development for middle management and faculty; Floyd and colleagues present leadership crises as potential opportunities for growth, and Cloud brings these many disparate change leadership experiences together and places them in an historical context.

Change leadership in contemporary community colleges is leadership that anticipates the future, analyzes the internal and external environment, acts by means of appropriate and timely data to ensure accountability while building on the strengths of its teams, and affirms and sustains change. In a time of limited resources and an uncertain economy, community colleges are more important than ever to meet the employment and educational needs of citizens in their communities. Visionary change leadership that sees beyond current dilemmas to a positive future will make the difference between those mediocre institutions that remain wedded to the old ways of managing and leading and those new stars that see opportunity in adversity and challenge and excitement in creating a culture of change in tomorrow's community colleges.

References

Beach, L. R. *Leadership and the Art of Change*. Thousand Oaks, Calif.: Sage, 2006.

Bennis, W. *On Becoming a Leader*. Reading, Mass.: Addison-Wesley, 1989.

Bennis, W., and Nanus, B. *Leaders: The Strategies for Taking Charge*. New York: Harper & Row, 1985.

Burke, W. W. *Organization Change: Theory and Practice*. Thousand Oaks, Calif.: Sage, 2008.

Cohen, M. D., and March, J. G. *Leadership and Ambiguity* (2nd ed.). Boston: Harvard Business School Press, 1986.

Cooper, R. K., and Sawaf, A. *Executive EQ: Emotional Intelligence in Leadership and Organizations*. New York: Penguin Putnam, 1997.

De Pree, M. *Leadership Is an Art*. New York: Doubleday, 1989.

Drucker, P. F. *Management Challenges for the 21st Century*. New York: HarperCollins, 1999.

Evans, R. "The Authentic Leader." In *Jossey-Bass Reader on Educational Leadership*. San Francisco: Jossey-Bass, 2000.

Fullan, M. *Leading in a Culture of Change*. San Francisco: Wiley, 2001.

Kotter, J. P. "What Leaders Really Do." In *Harvard Business Review on Leadership*. Boston: Harvard Business School, 1998, 37–60.

Lorenzo, A. L., and DeMarte, D. T. "Recruiting and Developing Leaders for the 21st Century." In D. Campbell (ed.), *The Leadership Gap*. Washington, D.C.: Community College Press, 2002.

Mintzberg, H. "The Manager's Job: Folklore and Fact." In *Harvard Business Review on Leadership*. Boston: Harvard Business School Press, 1998, 1–36.

Northouse, P. G. *Leadership: Theory and Practice*. Thousand Oaks, Calif.: Sage, 2007.

O'Banion, T. "New College Leaders Face Prickly New Dilemmas." *Community College Times*, Aug. 31, 2008. Retrieved July 7, 2009, from www.communitycollegetimes.com/article.cfm?ArticleID=1171.

Rath, T. *StrengthsFinder*. New York: Gallup, 2007.

Riggs, J. "Leadership, Change, and the Future of Community Colleges." *Academic Leadership*, Feb. 19, 2009. Retrieved July 6, 2009, from http://www.academicleadership.org/empirical_research/581_printer.shtml.

Roueche, J. E., Baker, G. A., and Rose, R. R. *Shared Vision: Transformational Leadership in American Community Colleges*. Washington, D.C.: Community College Press, 1989.

Senge, P., Scharmer, C. O., Jaworski, J., and Flowers, B. S. *Presence: Human Purpose and the Field of the Future*. Cambridge, Mass.: Society for Organizational Learning, 2004.
Tichy, N. M., and DeVanna, M. A. *The Transformational Leader*. New York: Wiley, 1990.
Wallin, D. L., and Ryan, J. R. "Order out of Chaos: Leadership for the 21st Century." *Community College Journal of Research and Practice*, 1994, 18(6), 527–538.
Wheatley, M. J. *Leadership and the New Science*. San Francisco: Berrett-Koehler, 1999.

DESNA L. WALLIN *is associate professor in the Department of Lifelong Education, Administration, and Policy at the University of Georgia and a former community college president in Iowa and North Carolina.*

NEW DIRECTIONS FOR COMMUNITY COLLEGES • DOI: 10.1002/cc

2

*One strategy used with increasing frequency to meet the
needs of multiple constituencies is partnerships and forms
of organizational collaboration, consortia, and networks.
This chapter explores the kinds of skills and thinking
required of community college leaders to engage in
effective partnerships.*

Leading Partnerships: Competencies for Collaboration

Marilyn J. Amey

Community colleges are constantly challenged to find new ways to meet the needs of multiple constituents. One strategy becoming more popular in addressing these pressing needs is partnerships and other forms of organizational collaboration, consortia, and networks. Partnerships can allow for resource sharing, creation of joint educational programs, technology enhancements, and workforce preparation. Expanded use of such collaborations leads to a greater need for people throughout the college to understand the nature of partnerships and the leadership required to effectively develop and sustain them.

Although these relationships may be sanctioned or initiated by college presidents, they are found throughout the college, with some personnel playing leadership roles. They may be defined as cross-unit or cross-institution, cross-town or cross-region, and even cross-country (or international). This chapter explores the kinds of thinking and skills required of community college leaders to engage in effective partnerships and discusses factors that affect the ongoing success of the collaborations. It will consider differences tied to partnership type and leadership position.

Defining Partnerships

We know that partnerships are becoming more common, often being encouraged by policy makers and grant funders (Amey, Eddy, and Ozaki, 2007). Even though the literature continues to develop, it is safe to say that

community college partnerships vary in their structure, complexity, duration, scope, clarity of roles and responsibilities, cost, and benefit to the college. What we know tends to focus, not surprisingly, on formal partnerships that are tightly coupled and highly structured, such as articulation agreements between community colleges and four-year institutions, dual-enrollment programs with public schools, some facilities-use agreements, and arrangements stipulated in state and federal legislation. Partnerships that are loosely coupled with informal structures may, in fact, be far more common and an outgrowth of formal associations or personal relationships between individuals. Yet, almost by definition, these arrangements are less likely to be written about and understood; it seems as if capturing them in print somehow moves the partnership toward more formalization. Interestingly, the success of informal partnerships may be based on the ability of these collaborations to fly under the bureaucratic radar. Such arrangements may include transition programming for students, site placements for internships in applied degree programs, K–12 classroom projects, and membership on advisory committees, among other variations.

Community college administrators and faculty can name many ways in which they link with public schools, local businesses and community agencies, universities, and other organizations. They can sometimes articulate the origins of these arrangements and who initiated them yet are often less able to identify the specific factors that lead to successful or effective partnerships and determine whether arrangements can be sustained in the long run. Conversely, in some instances there are longstanding relationships that defy institutional logic in explaining why they *have* lasted.

Why Partner?

Previous research shows that community colleges partner with other organizations for many reasons, among them facilities sharing, technology demands, state and institutional goal attainment, resource scarcity, teacher labor market constraints, and personal relationships between partners (Amey, Eddy, and Ozaki, 2007). As economies tighten and learning needs across sectors (including workforce training) increase, this list will undoubtedly expand. To think about what is needed to lead partnerships, however, requires considering the foundations for collaborative relationships so that the dynamics affecting leadership can be better understood.

One impetus often stated for cross-organizational relationships is for compliance and legislative reasons. Two examples of a legislative push for partnering are the Workforce Investment Act of 1998, which mandates that any entity receiving federal funds for adult education, literacy, and vocational education be an involved partner in a one-stop-center delivery system (Bragg and Russman, 2007), and the Carl D. Perkins Career and Technical Education Improvement Act of 2006, which supports career and technical education programs by encouraging student transition to college and entry into career as well as by promoting curriculum linkages to career pathways (Hull, 2005). Both federal policies require relationships across institutions and have become more central in recent years, not necessarily to the community college mission or to its leadership strategies but to individual states as they move more aggressively to stimulate movement (and inclusion) across educational pathways and improve workforce training and development in declining or transitioning economies (Farrell and Seifert, 2007; Kleinman, 2001).

States have their own versions of legislation that make it incumbent on community colleges to be willing and able to effectively partner with other organizations, including state-specific legislation related to dual enrollment and comprehensive student data record sharing (Farrell and Seifert, 2007). Community colleges have always been linking institutions across the educational spectrum, but increasingly they serve a broker role with a growing host of organizations. Knowing more about how partnerships evolve provides leverage for leaders to help support and maintain partnership development and potential sustainability. Various parts of the process may call for somewhat different leadership skills and thinking to be effectively and strategically implemented.

Understanding Partnerships

Several aspects of community college partnerships are important for leaders to consider: partnerships are very process oriented, they are not always rational, and those involved often have quite divergent motivations for participating.

Partnerships Are Process Oriented. They take time to unfold (Gray, 1989). It is important to recognize the value of various aspects of the partnership as it develops, rather than only focusing on the outputs. This can be a challenge for leaders in an era of increased accountability. Nevertheless, partnerships are often more important for the relationships they facilitate, the values they symbolize, and the political alliances that can be banked for future use than for the measurable outputs they produce, especially in the short run. For example, the goodwill generated through sharing health facilities between a community college and its neighbor public school may not produce substantial revenue, yet it can result in respect, information sharing, and trust among teachers and faculty that enhance transition advising for students between the high school and college. Likewise, partnering with social service agencies can afford greater access for college students to needed services, which may lead to increased retention and graduation rates.

Change leaders need to see how partnerships directly contribute to the college's mission and goal attainment in ways that reflect both quality and quantity; they need to look beyond the obvious outputs to less tangible outcomes such as bridges built that lead to success in other realms. This way of perceiving partnerships requires leaders to think systemically rather than just engage in rudimentary cost-benefit assessments, and to have a deeper understanding and valuing of the process nature of partnerships. It also requires an ability to lead in uncertain conditions because the process is constantly unfolding (Morgan, 2006).

Partnerships Are Nonrational. Leading partnerships requires recognizing that collaborations are often organized nonrationally, and so the leader needs to be comfortable with a level of ambiguity and dissonance (Morgan, 2006). This is not to say that partnerships are irrational, but they are not always linear and cannot just be mandated from the top. It is usually not enough to declare an arrangement to be a partnership and expect that the work will proceed in a very straightforward manner. Especially when working across educational institutions, leaders often ignore some of the fundamental differences between academic organizations (Amey, Eddy, and Ozaki, 2007). Organizational culture, reward systems, curricular structures, policy and decision-making involvement, funding, and time are just some of the issues that confront leaders when initiating educational partnerships across sectors. Areas of dissonance may be greater when community colleges partner with nonacademic organizations even though leaders seem to expect this more when partnering with other educational organizations. Studies have consistently shown that, even if formed by legislative action or institutional mandate, there are a lot of starts and stops as members establish common understanding of the partnership, articulate their motivations and goals for involvement, and develop shared language and processes (Amey and Brown, 2004; Hoffman-Johnson, 2007). Research also shows that the time required for these early formations is not typically included in funding cycles, roll-out plans, or calendars by which results are expected. As much as leaders need to set appropriate contexts and expectations for partnerships, they need to help those involved understand these same areas of ambiguity and development (Amey and Brown, 2004).

Partnerships Require Motivation. Motivations for participating vary, which means that understandings, commitment, resource distribution, and other features of the partnership vary as well (Eddy, 2003). They also change over time as the partnership evolves and as the partners themselves see the benefits and challenges of the collaboration more realistically. Therefore, stating the case for the partnership once and assuming that the message has "staying power" is naïve. A president may communicate to a partner in one way if the relationship is mandated or formed out of necessity and in another way if the partnership is perceived to be mutually beneficial and leading to positive outcomes. Additionally, leaders need to help campus members connect partnership work to their roles and responsibilities and give meaning to what they are doing. This is especially important if partnership goals change over time so that motivation can be maintained.

Skills in Leading Partnerships

Many of the skills needed for leading a partnership are similar to those required for leading a community college. Unlike leading a college, however, partnerships may be managed by those at the top or those located elsewhere in the organization. Senior leaders need to realize they are not alone in facilitating aspects of partnership development. Similarly, midlevel leaders need to understand the critical role they play in both building collaborations and sustaining the work.

Communication. In every organization, including a cross-sector educational collaboration, members need to understand the motivation behind and benefits of the partnership. At the level of partnership implementation, there are pragmatic questions that need answers and clear communication with campus members. Some of these questions: What does it mean for the community college and other organizations to pursue a similar goal? How do the partners need to interact to accomplish that goal? Who pays? Who gets paid? Because it is a similar goal, will each partner benefit equally? These questions need clarification, at least in the beginning, for the partnership to proceed. How partnerships are presented on and off campus affects how they are perceived by others, so skills in framing and communicating about partnerships are critical (Amey, Eddy, and Ozaki, 2007; Eddy, 2003). Effective and consistent communication helps establish the context, clarifies goals and objectives, and creates common vocabulary and understandings. It also takes into account the perspectives partners bring to the relationships, helping keep members informed and focused on the future and helping them solve problems more effectively (Gray, 1989).

Because partnerships almost always draw on existing educational resources, even when new resources are initially available from seed money or grant funds, members need to see the partnership as value-added and not drawing off other college priorities. Knowing how they will benefit is a prime motivator for participants—the age old question, "What's in it for my organization?" If this is clearly communicated by a senior leader or champion located elsewhere in the college, commitment is higher, motivation is sustained, and creative strategies for accomplishing goals are developed rather than members engaging in defensive posturing and "turf protecting."

As the partnership evolves through the developmental stages and inherent structural and personnel difficulties common in cross-institutional efforts, the need to explain the collaboration and clarify work and benefits is ongoing and demands adequate attention (Eddy, 2003). Leaders have to look for, create, or seize opportunities to celebrate partnership successes and to highlight and showcase effective examples, outcomes, and strategies; for instance, agreement signing and ribbon-cutting ceremonies for new partnerships open to the public show the symbolic value of the collaborative work and invite constituents to feel part of the process from the beginning (Amey and Brown, 2004). Milestone updates in publications and newsletters to school families connect them to the partnerships and maintain visibility, which can be important when involvement or assistance is needed. Yet leaders need to be careful not to shift the ownership away from members and to themselves as a central, leader-owned initiative. Moving from a shared partnership to a single-leader-focused initiative adds an authoritarian dynamic and stifles motivation to participate and potential for group ownership of the process.

Consistent messages over time are also critical for maintaining a sense of purpose for the partnership. Leaders have to create widespread commitment beyond core relationships, so they need to understand how and when to broaden bases of support for educational partnerships. This includes building commitment in those constituents less directly involved in a specific partnership, such as parents, teachers, faculty, school boards, or business leaders, who constitute another prime audience because they can undermine, vote against, or lend additional support to the partnership depending on how they understand it. Being aware of communication strategies and how messages are interpreted is therefore useful. These communication and support-building responsibilities are not the job only of college presidents, even though much credence is often given when presidents comment on various partnership initiatives in state-of-the-college addresses, podcasts, and internal communiqués.

Organizational Analysis. In considering beginning a partnership, leaders need to become effective organizational analysts to determine viable relationships that are productive for the college and the prospective partner. Relevant questions include but are not limited to these: Why should the college partner? What are its strengths? How should the other organizational partner be assessed, and what does it bring to the relationship? Asking questions may be framed as a kind of organizational data-based decision making, or as assessing the cost and benefits of the relationship, and requires being able to see both the partnership and the larger organizations for what they are and what they may become together. Doing so implies a deep understanding of the college or units within it, its current status and future growth capacity, and the kind of strategy that is most beneficial in the short and long run (Cameron, 1984). This kind of analysis suggests that leaders have to be at very senior levels of the college to have sufficient breadth of understanding and organizational perspective. Yet many creative partnerships are established by those in lower levels of the institution because employees have more direct knowledge of unit potential when in proximity to the work and may also be more familiar with areas that will require support if the partnership is to be successful, such as a need for released time, training, or additional resources. No matter where they are located within the college, those leading partnerships must read the organization's climate, needs, and readiness for change accurately to know whether engaging in partnerships will be beneficial (Handy, 2002).

Organizational analysts also need to consider unintended outcomes of the partnership that may be positive (such as changed institutional culture and faculty reward system) or negative (time lost for other important activities, increased competition for funds). Potential unintended consequences may have as great an impact as the stated goals of the partnership over the long run (Handy, 2002). As important as having credible longitudinal impact data is, leaders must realize that systems, including partnerships, evolve over time; they must be willing to modify stated objectives, data collected, and ways of communicating about these collaborations as needed.

Group Facilitation Skills. Similar to team development, partnership development can be helped to move from just a coordinated effort that is most likely to fall apart at the first significant challenge to collaboration where goals are mutually understood, members are invested in each other as well as in the outcome, and the partnership becomes institutionalized, if this is the goal (Amey and Brown, 2004). It is important to distinguish early on between short-term, situation-specific collaborations and those intended to be long term. The differences in support, resource needs, buy-in, structure, and leadership can be dramatic and have to be understood by those trying to facilitate the partnership.

In the early stages of a partnership, relationships are the key to getting the program going. Leaders play a central role in how these relationships are cultivated, structured, and operated. Building trust among players is paramount (Leveille, 2006), and negotiating the relationships needs to come more from a mutual-gains perspective if there is any hope the partnership will be retained over time, even if partners do not benefit in the same ways or to the same extent (Morgan, 2006). In addition to ways of thinking about partnerships already mentioned, those leading or championing the cause need to recognize that their own roles within the group process will evolve as well as the partnership develops from coordinated to collaborative. Initially, as with any group, it is sometimes necessary for leaders to be more leader-centered, using top-down management controls. Yet, over time as the partnership evolves, stabilizes, and becomes more institutionalized, ownership of the idea and involvement of others must be expanded into forms of distributed leadership (Amey and Brown, 2004). Without this shift in role and responsibility, the partnership stays too closely associated with the single leader, and investment over time will have to be coerced more than it will be freely given.

It is not always clear whether this shift in role from the single champion to the partnership facilitator will be accepted practice in each partner institution and for each champion, and so may confound the change in leader role (Amey and Brown, 2004). For example, college constituents may become suspect if a president is no longer talking regularly about a particular initiative she once vocally championed. Leaders need to help others find their voice in speaking for and framing partnerships as roles change and champions emerge. There is also a question of timing in that if a leadership change in the partnership occurs too soon—before partners are prepared or the relationship is secure enough to weather the transition—the partnership can destabilize and potentially even dissolve (Amey and Brown,

2004). Passing on credibility for leading is part of the shift necessary for institutionalizing and sustaining partnerships, and if the process is complicated on one's campus, astute communication and leadership skills will be required to handle things effectively.

Differences Across Partnership Context and Leadership Position

It is important to identify factors that influence or mediate partnerships in their various configurations to provide for better decision making, policy development, and strategic planning as well as for more longstanding collaborations. Articulation agreements, transfer and credit evaluations, equipment- and facilities-use agreements, funding regulations, and field-specific professional standards often furnish formal standards and guidelines for how partners will work together to achieve shared goals. By contrast, less-formal partnerships typically require more negotiation before roles and responsibilities are established among members. Differences in type of system involved in the partnership affect the relationship even if both are educational organizations. K–12 schools and community colleges, for example, have quite different structures for faculty appointments and work hours, contract stipulations (or lack of contract), governance and decision-making purview, and ways of functioning that may potentially affect partnerships. These contextual distinctions need to be understood by leaders and common ground must be established if trusting relationships are to be established and effective partnerships developed (Amey, Eddy, and Ozaki, 2007; Sink and Jackson, 2002).

Position. Cross-sector educational partnerships require champions to (1) create the vision that establishes the need for the partnership, (2) shepherd processes, (3) ensure buy-in, (4) communicate goals and outcomes, and (5) generate and maintain a high level of commitment to the activity. The leader/champion is typically a key communicator, resource broker, and partnership facilitator. Champions must have passion for the partnership because these relationships are not always easy to develop or considered part of a person's assigned work. Personal passion, including the sense of a moral imperative built on core values of community colleges to serve local learner needs, can be a compelling motivator for those who champion partnerships, perhaps much more so than implementing the directives of a passionate supervisor or president. These differences are important to consider because they may have an impact later on for faculty and administrative structures, how resources flow and from where, and how the original intent of the partnership can be effectively managed over time.

The literature (for example, Kotter and Cohen, 2002) suggests the importance of senior-level buy-in, as by college presidents. Yet in most academic organizations, senior leaders are not likely to be involved in actually implementing the partnership, so whether they serve as champion or "just" ensure resource allocation is not clear. It is equally likely that others within the organization are leading the partnership and cultivating the support of those in more formal authority. This kind of diffusion of innovation throughout the college (and its partner) puts leadership in the hands of those most closely associated with the work and the outcomes. Many partnerships are spearheaded by senior administrators (presidents, college deans, program directors), who then are sure to bring others on board, including midlevel administrators and faculty, to take on daily implementation and decision making associated with the partnership. There are clear advantages to moving partnership activities closer to the front lines, but it also leaves the potential for time gaps and communication problems between organizational levels that may jeopardize relationships in difficult economic situations or when those most familiar are not structurally part of the decision-making body. Judicious monitoring of these relationships and communication strategies by leaders at all levels is warranted.

As noted, champions do not have to be college presidents, although presidential support is critically important in securing the resources necessary to establish partnerships. At the same time, partnerships are at risk if they become too closely aligned with any one person, group, funding source, or political agenda. This can be seen clearly and become quite challenging if the champion leaves the college without getting significant buy-in from others for the partnership. To be sustained, partnerships must become institutionalized to be valued by more than the champion, if in fact sustainability is a goal.

That those who champion partnerships can be located throughout the college raises the notion of different forms of capital, including power, relationship and information networks, and resources (Coleman, 1998; Morgan, 2006). Presidents typically have the necessary political collateral and resource control to achieve college goals, including those associated with any number of partnerships. However, champions throughout the college have their own forms of capital that may be important to implementing and sustaining effective partnerships. Negotiations that support partnerships may be small in scale and rely most heavily on interpersonal connections and social capital. Large-scale partnerships may draw on a broad range of relationships and resources, so they may typically need the support of those with more and different forms of capital to invest.

There is no inherent concern in the distribution of capital among champions; however, it is quite possible that champions from partner organizations may have their own forms of capital at their disposal that are more or less relevant, more or less plentiful, and more or less within their individual jurisdiction to use (Morgan, 2006; Watson, 2007). One needs to be mindful of potential uneven power bases between partners making the partnership far more beneficial to one player or organization than the other. Enthusiasm is important but insufficient for moving the partnership through developmental stages to full enactment and potential sustainability. The right resources at the right time spent in the right way can make the difference between success and failure, even with the best of intentions (Amey and Brown, 2004).

Conclusion and Implications for Practice

In sum, partnership may be a very effective strategy for a community college to broaden outreach and build the capacity to achieve stated organizational goals, especially when resources are tight and learner needs are growing. From a change leadership perspective, several aspects of these relationships need to be considered, especially if the eventual goal is for the partnership to become part of the ongoing work of the college.

- Partnerships are difficult and complex. They rely on the interplay of numerous actors with their own motivations and goals. They do not just happen because policy makers, boards of trustees, or even college presidents mandate they will occur.
- Partnerships, like other groups and forms of organizations, evolve through stages and thus have differing leadership and resource needs over time.
- How people understand the intent and goals of the partnership is critical to its success. Leaders have to frame the partnership for others effectively and recognize that how they communicate about the collaboration will likely change as it evolves.
- Leading partnerships requires being an effective organizational analyst and systems thinker, knowing the strengths and challenges of one's organization, and understanding how partnering will be of benefit.
- Partnerships are typically quite labor-intensive, at least during the relationship-building phase. It takes time to develop trust, determine roles and responsibilities, and build effective working relationships.
- Leader-centered partnerships are often less likely to be sustained over time than those that have become more inclusive. Leaders need to know when and how to broaden commitment and involvement and to step aside so that other champions can continue implementation of the partnership.

References

Amey, M. J., and Brown, D. F. *Breaking Out of the Box: Interdisciplinary Collaboration and Faculty Work.* Boston: Information Age, 2004.

Amey, M. J., Eddy, P. L., and Ozaki, C. C. "Demands for Partnership and Collaboration in Higher Education: A Model." In M. J. Amey (ed.), *Collaborations Across Educational Sectors.* New Directions for Community Colleges, no. 139. San Francisco: Jossey-Bass, 2007.

Bragg, D. D., and Russman, M. L. "The Legislative Playing Field: How Public Policy Influences Collaboration." In M. J. Amey (ed.), *Collaborations Across Educational Sectors.* New Directions for Community Colleges, no. 139. San Francisco: Jossey-Bass, 2007.

Cameron, K. S. "Organizational Adaptation and Higher Education." *Journal of Higher Education,* 1984, 55(2), 122–144.

Coleman, J. S. "Social capital in the creation of human capital." *The American Journal of Sociology*, 1988, 94, S95–S120.

Eddy, P. L. "Sensemaking on Campus: How Community College Presidents Frame Change." *Community College Journal of Research and Practice*, 2003, 27(6), 453–471.

Farrell, P. L., and Seifert, K. A. "Lessons Learned from a Dual-Enrollment Partnership." In M. J. Amey (ed.), *Collaborations Across Educational Sectors*. New Directions for Community Colleges, no. 139. San Francisco: Jossey-Bass, 2007.

Gray, B. *Collaborating: Finding Common Ground for Multiparty Problems*. San Francisco: Jossey-Bass, 1989.

Handy, C. "Elephants and Fleas: Is Your Organization Prepared for Change?" *Leader to Leader Journal*, 2002, 24.

Hoffman-Johnson, G. "Seamless Transition in the Twenty-First Century: Partnering to Survive and Thrive." In M. J. Amey (ed.), *Collaborations Across Educational Sectors*. New Directions for Community Colleges, no. 139. San Francisco: Jossey-Bass, 2007.

Hull, D. "Career Pathways: Education with a Purpose." In D. Hull (ed.), *Career Pathways: Education with a Purpose*. Waco, Texas: Center for Occupational Research and Development, 2005.

Kleinman, N. S. *Building a Highway to Higher Education: How Collaborative Efforts Are Changing Education in America*. New York: Center for Urban Future, 2001.

Kotter, J. P., and Cohen, D. S. *The Heart of Change: Real Life Stories of How People Change Their Organizations*. Cambridge, Mass.: Harvard Business School Press, 2002.

Leveille, D. E. *Accountability in Higher Education: A Public Agenda for Trust and Cultural Change*. Research and Occasional Paper Series. Berkeley: Center for Studies in Higher Education, University of California, Berkeley, 2006.

Morgan, G. *Images of Organizations* (2nd ed.). Beverly Hills, Calif.: Sage, 2006.

Sink, D. W., and Jackson, K. L. "Successful Community College Campus-Based Partnerships." *Community College Journal of Research and Practice*, 2002, 26(1), 35–46.

Watson, J. S. "Stepping Outside the Big Box High School: A Partnership Influenced by Goals, Capital, and Decision Making." In M. J. Amey (ed.), *Collaborations Across Educational Sectors*. New Directions for Community Colleges, no. 139. San Francisco: Jossey-Bass, 2007.

MARILYN J. AMEY *is professor and chair of the Department of Educational Administration at Michigan State University.*

3

Leaders and managers in community colleges need to be flexible in their everyday job roles and responsibilities. Teams are widely used to serve specific purposes in community college administration. Adopting the research of several Harvard scholars, the authors remind community college administrators when creating dynamic teams to keep a careful balance of leaders and managers.

Dynamic Leadership Development in Community College Administration: Theories, Applications, and Implications

Matthew J. Basham, Raghu P. Mathur

As the twenty-first century progresses, educators face considerable turmoil from the economy, shrinking budgets, aging facilities, and high turnover and attrition among employees at all levels, all the while contending with increasing enrollments and a declining completion rate. These challenges don't even include the ever-growing number of students arriving at the school doors who are not fully prepared to begin their education at a community college without first receiving remediation. Within this climate, job roles and responsibilities of leaders and managers are stretched beyond the boundaries of their traditional descriptions. More often, the skills and talents of leaders and managers fall into the "other duties as assigned" function. One such duty for community college leaders and managers is serving on a variety of administrative teams. In many instances ongoing or static teams can become stale and fizzle or lose their potential to be productive. Instead, dynamic teams may serve the institution much better by delivering a better product and being more useful through developing the skills and talents of their leaders and managers. This requires further development and refinement of leadership and management traits within those teams to more fully and capably address these challenges and opportunities. These seemingly dual abilities, having appropriately fine-tuned leadership and management skills, will therefore make for better employees all around.

25

NEW DIRECTIONS FOR COMMUNITY COLLEGES, no. 149, Spring 2010 © 2010 Wiley Periodicals, Inc.
Published online in Wiley InterScience (www.interscience.wiley.com) • DOI: 10.1002/cc.392

Theories

Before discussing the applications and implications for dynamic teams in community colleges, this section includes a review of the applicable literature on teams as well as defining leaders and managers as they pertain to administration.

"Team" Theories. Scholars of teams and team analysis point to Kotter's body of work. Kotter has spent many years working with corporate entities and Fortune 1,000 companies to assess their leadership strengths and to expose their weaknesses. From this research he has produced numerous theories, models, and practical applications, one of which involves creating good teams. Kotter's theory on teams plots the leadership assessment score versus the management assessment score. From this plot he can deduce which teams are good, bad, and somewhat bad but "could be good with some tweaking."

> Four key characteristics seem to be essential to effective guiding coalitions. They are: (1) *Position Power:* are enough key players on board, especially the main line managers, so that those left out cannot easily block progress? (2) *Expertise:* are the various points of view, in terms of discipline, work experience, nationality, etc., relevant to the task at hand adequately represented so that informed, intelligent decisions will be made? (3) *Credibility:* does the group have enough people with good reputations in the firm so that its pronouncements will be taken seriously by the other employees? (4) *Leadership:* does the group include enough proven leaders to be able to drive the change process? [Kotter, 1996, p. 58].

Teams top-heavy with leaders will produce plenty of direction but generally stall without managers to take care of the details and keep the project moving along. On the other hand, teams top-heavy with managers will be good at filling out forms and following the procedures, but without direction and vision they will not help the organization grow. This type of team will "control rather than empower people" (Kotter, 1996, p. 58). Finally, teams lacking both leaders and managers will produce little growth, if any.

Defining "Leaders." Conducting an academic search of the term *leader* reveals thousands of articles. When asked to define the ideal leader, many would emphasize traits such as intelligence, toughness, determination, flexibility, and vision. Often left off the list are softer, more personal, but still essential qualities: "Leadership defines what the future should look like, aligns people with that vision, and inspires them to make it happen, despite the obstacles" (Kotter, 1996, p. 25). Although a certain degree of analytical and technical skill is a minimum requirement for success, studies indicate that emotional intelligence may be a key attribute that distinguishes outstanding performers from those who are merely "adequate." Goleman (2004) found truly effective leaders to be distinguished by a high degree of emotional intelligence. Without it, a person can have first-class training, an incisive mind, and an endless supply of good ideas, but he or she still will

NEW DIRECTIONS FOR COMMUNITY COLLEGES • DOI: 10.1002/cc

not be a great leader. The chief components of emotional intelligence are self-awareness, self-regulation, motivation, empathy, and social skills. Again, the softer, more personal qualities set great leaders apart from good leaders. Leaders with these qualities are better positioned as change leaders in community colleges. Other researchers (see, for example, Doh, 2003; or Goffee and Jones, 2004) have found similar results.

Defining Managers. As with defining leadership, finding a common definition of *manager* or *management* is just as problematic. Kotter (1996) defines the latter as "a set of processes that can keep a complicated system of people and technology running smoothly" (p. 25). Managers, he says, are those people who are good at following steps one through ten to accomplish the objectives of the business. Leaders, on the other hand, develop new processes when steps one through ten are not working efficiently.

An Aside: Career Paths. Some conclusions can be drawn from the literature and the Kotter model about the potential career paths of aspiring leaders and managers. An average person right out of college will usually not possess a skill set of strong leadership or management skills. As this person grows and develops into a career path, he or she would tend to be given more management responsibilities early and leadership roles later in his or her career. Of course, at any point a person may become comfortable and not wish to advance any further, but for the sake of argument it is assumed the young manager wishes to go all the way to the top of the administrative chain. As he or she climbs the career ladder, roles and responsibilities shift away from management-oriented tasks and skills to more leadership-oriented tasks. Depending on the size of the community college and the position, it is assumed that management skills decline as more leadership tasks are assumed. Should the leader preside over a smaller community college, he or she would naturally expect to wear many hats and, consequently, retain more of his or her management skills. Such leaders also tend to fall into the "healer" category since they need to maintain those interpersonal skills and close relationships with even the lowest person on the academic ladder. Conversely, the leader of a larger community college would tend to retain fewer management skills since he or she typically has more staff to whom to delegate assignments. These leaders also tend to fall into the "change agent" category of leader espoused in the literature since creating change drives the ascent to the top of the career ladder.

This article develops application of those theories in practical settings for community college administrators in an environment of change.

Applications

Use of assessments for a variety of purposes in community colleges has increasingly emerged as a topic of discussion over the past few years. Not surprisingly, this topic has seemingly coincided with the emergence of the literature on the waves of turnover and attrition taking place in community colleges. Assessments have many uses in the workplace, among them as revenue-generating instruments (Mendoza, Basham, Campbell, et al., 2009), in the hiring process, for personnel and career development, and in creating benchmarks (Basham, 2007; Basham, 2008; Krell, 2005). Assessments can also be used, in conjunction with all of the above, for developing effective dynamic teams and creating dynamic team benchmarks.

More than three thousand assessments are available for use in the United States, yet public and private foundations are still channeling millions of dollars into developing new assessments. Are these assessments not valid or reliable? Many of them are both. Are they too costly? Many cost less than a hundred dollars each. Do they not fit the need? You can find many assessments to meet specific needs, whether blue-collar or white-collar, from janitors to CEOs. It makes little sense to continue developing new instruments. Instead, the researchers suggest using an existing form in newer applications such as dynamic team assessment. By using assessments to gauge the benchmarks, strengths, and weaknesses of employees, the employer will have more data available to drive forward innovation and ideals as a change leader.

Using Assessments in Team Analysis

The literature contains many references to "these" traits for leaders and "those" traits for managers. We attempted to divide the assessment characteristics into mutually exclusive traits for leaders and managers. This task, however, proved too difficult since managers and leaders share traits (although some scores differ for leaders and managers). For example, leaders tend to be a bit more conceptual than managers, which seems to follow the literature in that managers are not as well skilled at providing conceptual ideas and visions but are more adept at keeping projects on task. Therefore we suggest that future research use the benchmarks (the average scores) for community college administrators or more finite subdivisions (such as creating benchmarks for deans or program directors). The benchmarks are not indicators of future success, but rather just a gauge of what traits past employees had in those positions to possibly help identify the best fit. Consequently, this research is a starting point.

Implications for Practitioners

Assessment data are one of the most cost-effective methods available to assist in selecting leaders and managers, especially in medium to large organizations. A bad fit between an administrator and an institution can take a toll on careers and families alike. The months invested in mentoring and coaching to improve the performance of those members of a dynamic team can bring frustration and anxiety if a candidate does not fulfill expectations. The staff surrounding the underperforming employee may have to endure heavier workloads, and resentment toward the employee or administration

NEW DIRECTIONS FOR COMMUNITY COLLEGES • DOI: 10.1002/cc

may build. Eventually the underperforming employee may be dismissed. Even with the most amicable separation, however, there may be a substantial financial toll, legal fees, settlement costs, and the equally devastating and frustrating loss of time and productivity in having to search again for a new candidate for that position. The ability to make a right decision in hiring may be greatly enhanced with assessment data; a good hiring decision is always more cost-effective than a mismatch.

Dynamic leadership to meet today's challenges requires adaptability to change and the capacity to lead and manage change. Assessment data can help to identify those attributes for hiring decisions, as well as identify the capacity for development in those dynamic teams. Leaders must create dynamic teams that stretch typical job descriptions. More cross-functional and multidisciplinary teams are now being led by nontraditional leaders. For instance, target-marketing teams may be led by staff who are not the most seasoned leaders but best represent the target generation (gen Y, gen X, boomer, and so on). They are chosen to lead from their direct experience and to consider them for future leadership opportunities. Dynamic teams stray from the traditional wisdom of having the most experienced leader in charge of a team, relying instead on subject matter experts who have some modicum of leadership aptitude to lead the team. Those seasoned leaders can then assume a mentor-style role to assist the dynamic team leader when asked. The mentor role will also heighten the credibility of the seasoned leader, who may be seen as a good follower as well.

The cost of making a bad decision in a hiring process can be significant. Using assessments to assist in the hiring process can help diminish this possibility and can also assist in creating dynamic teams in a way not traditionally used in community college administration. Managers must be willing to see the big picture of an organization and implement managerial tasks to fulfill that mission to better serve students. Without a clearly articulated vision from well-trained leaders, this will not happen. Leaders and managers serving on dynamic teams will help to create a communication conduit leading to the cohesiveness necessary to drive forward the mission of the institution. Finally, a traditional team may not be able to function well in today's environment absent a careful balance of leaders and managers, causing the team to "fizzle" in their output. Using dynamic teams, constantly building the leadership and management skills, and identifying the best possible individuals for the team according to the task will create "sizzle" for the institution.

Limitations and Suggestions for Future Research

There are limitations to this research. Using assessments to connect theory to practice has been scarce in community college administration research; difficulties are encountered if not all members of the team complete their assessments; assessments do not always help to identify the diamonds in the rough; and there has been very little research on the statistical soundness of these suggested applications.

First, this is an attempt to apply the literature of the Harvard scholars to community college administration leadership and management measurement using assessments for the purpose of creating dynamic teams through data-driven decision making. The next logical step would be to calculate the benchmark scores of various administrative teams from a number of community colleges and present a discussion of those results on the basis of creation of their teams. This would help drive the connection between research and practice.

Second, the continuing research suggested through assessing administrators may be difficult to conduct. Although cost-effective and scientifically valid and reliable assessments are available, community college administrators may be reluctant to use them. In confidential conversation, administrators noted several problems with adopting this type of research. If the assessments on administrative teams find someone who is clearly below all established benchmarks for his or her position, what is the obligation? Sometimes not knowing is better, especially if appointments to positions are political, family-related, or otherwise unrelated to the skills and talents of the applicant.

Third, especially in larger schools and multicampus colleges, this research could be especially valuable to the administration in helping to identify any undiscovered talent. These may be people who are normally not considered because of shyness or past differences of opinion with administration or middle managers, or some administrator may see the talent potential but feel threatened. Anderson and Kilduff's study (as cited in Kluger, 2009) on leadership of teams found the more vocal people with the most ideas often appeared to be seen as competent leaders. In fact, the study showed that often they were not the best ones to lead the team but just the most vocal. In any case, for a chancellor or president, using assessments can serve as a good check on the analysis and reasoning of the senior administrative team.

Fourth, future research could focus on validation of statistical analysis of the data. What is the relationship between assessment scores and job performance? Is there a standard correlation range in the Kotter model for community college administration? From the model it appears the better teams in the plot will statistically correlate closer to a value of 1 (a tighter cluster around a plotted line from the lower-left corner to the upper-right corner) while a poorer team will statistically correlate closer to a value of 0 (no cluster). This represents an area for further study as well.

Fifth, once benchmarks are created and individuals and teams are assessed, how do those findings hold longitudinally? The team may appear to be good on paper, but did the team actually accomplish the tasks in a timely and efficient manner? Do they do so repeatedly? What are the derailers encountered? Perhaps someone appeared to be good on paper, but on a team the person constantly showed up late. Assessments may not always

NEW DIRECTIONS FOR COMMUNITY COLLEGES • DOI: 10.1002/cc

catch the intangibles. This research is meant to impart some structure during these turbulent times, where very little may exist. Most of all this research should help to more effectively promote the mission and vision of an institution and help with succession planning and change leadership development efforts.

Conclusion

There may be a better way to assess and improve employees to create more effective dynamic teams; however, the literature offers few suggestions. Using assessments to build dynamic teams can foster greater success in creating a team to improve curriculum offerings, creating new visions or directions for the institution, or even in helping to drive a quality-enhancement planning team. This data-driven decision-making model surely will be critical in helping to navigate difficult economic times during a period of high turnover and attrition. Many teams in community college administration are composed of members who appear to be competent; but how does the president really know that an institution has the right balance of people? How does one really know that the team is giving maximum effort? Does a team leader feel confident that all the information needed from subordinates to select or approve team composition is available? Perhaps there is doubt from time to time, which could be removed simply by using low-cost assessments.

A good, dynamic team may be short-lived or serve a longer tenure. The key to creating effective dynamic teams is not to assemble teams with the most popular or most vocal individuals, but do so according to the specific purposes of the team and with the best individuals possible. Assessments may help to deduce the best fit for creating the team to maximize the sizzle. Finally, research suggests the importance of incorporating position power, expertise, credibility, and change leadership to produce an effective, dynamic team.

References

Anderson, C., and Kilduff, G. J. "Why Do Dominant Personalities Attain Influence in Face-to-Face Groups? The Competence-Signaling Effects of Trait Dominance." *Journal of Personality and Social Psychology,* 2009, *96,* 491–503.

Basham, M. J. "A Quantitative Study Examining Entrepreneurialism of NCCET Members." *Catalyst,* 2008, *37*(3), 3–7.

Basham, M. J. "A Cognitive Application of Personality Testing: Measuring Entrepreneurialism in America's Community Colleges." Unpublished doctorate dissertation, College of Education, University of Florida, 2007.

Basham, M. J., Campbell, D. F., and Mendoza, P. "Critical Issues Facing America's Community Colleges: A Summary of the Community College Futures Assembly 2008." *Community College Journal of Research and Practice,* 2008, *32*(11), 857–870.

Basham, M. J., Stader, D., and Bishop, H. B. "How Pathetic Is Your Hiring Process? An Application of the Lessig 'Pathetic Dot' Model to Educational Hiring Practices." *Community College Journal of Research and Practice,* 2009, *33*(3–4), 363–385.

Doh, J. P. "Can Leadership Be Taught?" *Academy of Management Learning and Education,* 2003, *2*(1), 54–67.

Drucker, P. "The Discipline of Innovation." *Harvard Business Review*, 1998, Nov.–Dec., 149–157.

Goffee, R., and Jones, G. "What Makes a Leader?" *Business Strategy Review*, 2004, 15(2), 46–50.

Goleman, D. "What Makes a Leader?" *Harvard Business Review*, 2004, 82(1), 82–91.

Kluger, J. "Is Your Boss Faking It?" Retrieved Mar. 2, 2009, from http://www.time.com/time/health/article/0,8599,1878358,00.html.

Kotter, J. P. *Leading Change*. Boston: Harvard Business School Press, 1996.

Krell, E. "Personality Counts: Personality Assessments Are Being Used in New Ways Through the Employee Life Cycle." *HR Magazine*, 2005, 50(11), 46–53.

Mendoza, P., Basham, M., and Campbell, D., et al. "Missions, Values, and 'Flying Monkeys': Critical Issues For Community Colleges Today and in 2019." *Community College Journal of Research and Practice*, 2009, 33(11), 866–882.

O'Daniels, K. M. "An Examination of Leadership Traits by Gender in Community College Administration." Unpublished doctoral dissertation, College of Education, University of Florida, 2009.

MATTHEW J. BASHAM is assistant professor in the Department of Educational Leadership and Policy Studies at the University of Texas-Arlington.

RAGHU P. MATHUR is chancellor of the South Orange County Community College District.

NEW DIRECTIONS FOR COMMUNITY COLLEGES • DOI: 10.1002/cc

4

This chapter describes the development of a community college leadership program that integrates interpersonal competency building with the process of personality and work-style profiling and individualized instruction in targeted areas for improvement.

Minding the Gap: Filling a Void in Community College Leadership Development

Dale F. Campbell, Syraj Syed, Phillip A. Morris

The end of the twentieth century heralded a period of anxiety among community college trustees and leaders over impending shortfalls in leadership positions. The tremendous growth of public community colleges in the 1960s made them particularly susceptible to the retirement of aging baby boomers. To assist in developing and selecting professionals to address this gap, the 21st Century Educational Leadership Profiles Project was created (Campbell and Leverty, 1997). This project aimed to increase the understanding of leadership attributes and the work styles of successful college presidents, particularly in an environment that requires skills in management of change.

Attribute-based person-job match reports, with key work-style profiles identified for community college leaders, were created for the community college presidents in the study sample. Additionally, these tools can also be used effectively in community colleges for professional development, as well as for ensuring an excellent personality-environment fit for institutional hiring processes. Work-styles questionnaires, such as the Occupational Personality Questionnaire (OPQ), which is the industry standard used by more than a thousand corporations worldwide, are used in executive selection, development, and succession planning.

Through the work of the Profiles Project and ongoing research at the University of Florida's Institute for Higher Education (Campbell, 2006),

New Directions for Community Colleges, no. 149, Spring 2010 © 2010 Wiley Periodicals, Inc.
Published online in Wiley InterScience (www.interscience.wiley.com) • DOI: 10.1002/cc.393

the value-added dimension of using the OPQ has been recognized as it contributes to translation of work styles (preferred individual and team styles) into competencies. For example, the OPQ can be used to assess managerial, professional, entrepreneurial, and personal qualities.

This effort was predicated on the conceptual framework that community college leadership development occurs in three strands:

1. The discipline (profession or practice) of community college leadership through traditional coursework (essential components in any higher education leadership program, such as finance, law, or policy)
2. Inquiry-based rationale building through research and data analysis coursework and the dissertation-writing process (also required in traditional program plans)
3. Development of interpersonal competencies through the process of personality and work-style profiling and executive coaching in targeted areas of improvement

The third component focuses on the widening gap in most leadership development curricula. Goleman (1998) suggests that truly effective leaders are distinguished by a high degree of emotional intelligence. Emotional intelligence comprises the attributes of self-awareness, self-regulation, motivation, empathy, and social interaction. Though analytical and reasoning skill sets are essential for leadership success, Goleman suggests that what truly distinguishes "outstanding" leaders from "average" ones is a higher degree of emotional intelligence.

Leadership coursework typically exposes students to instruments that measure personality type and style assessments. Though such assessment tools may assist in team building, many do not have sufficient validity to be included as a component of the hiring practice, and the results are not useful in identifying specific adjustments necessary for individual development of students' preferred work styles and habits.

Facilitating improvements in emotional intelligence cannot be achieved via a stand-alone course. Significant change in preferred work styles can occur only through a sustained and systematic effort. Students can assess and determine their level of competency in a semester-based course, but true mastery and behavioral change requires time, ongoing commitment to the process, executive coaching, and support.

Faced with the need to change, individuals often fail to follow through with the commitment to change (Deutschman, 2007). The goal in this chapter is to document acknowledgment of this gap in traditional leadership programs and to describe ways to implement targeted improvements in essential interpersonal competencies for future leaders. This chapter can then serve as a practical model for leadership development programs that can be replicated and researched by other programs.

NEW DIRECTIONS FOR COMMUNITY COLLEGES • DOI: 10.1002/cc

Leadership Competencies Building

In support of development of community college leadership, the American Association of Community Colleges (AACC) collaborated extensively with its partners to identify emergent themes that translated into valuable competencies for community college leaders:

- Organizational strategy
- Resource management
- Communication
- Collaboration
- Advocacy
- Professionalism

The Institute of Higher Education continued its research on leader profiles on a parallel track to the work of AACC, yielding an attribute-based person-job match report. This report generated nineteen characteristics, ranked as essential, important, or relevant other, for the community college president in a competitive environment. Three essential characteristics (data rational, critical, and forward planning) especially reflect the essence of what AACC deems the foundation of effective leadership.

The initial research of the 21st Century Leader Profiles Project led to a strand of inquiry into leadership competencies and impending leadership shortages. In 2002 member colleges of the Profiles Project came together to publish *The Leadership Gap*, a collection of model strategies for leadership selection and development for community colleges (Campbell, 2002).

Another phase of the research in 2006 found that retirement was going to have a major impact on specialized administrative positions such as college registrar and financial aid director (Campbell, 2006). The research also suggested that the skills and competencies required for specialized administrative positions were changing and expanding. Understanding the shortages that exist and the skills required for these leadership positions is a critical task for leadership academies. Through partnerships with community colleges and professional organizations, university leadership development programs can provide graduate and certificate programs targeted at expanding the skills necessary for specialized positions and can fill the gap within these fields.

Learning Outcomes and Learning Gains

Tunks (2007) and Salvano (2005) conducted their doctoral dissertations on the effectiveness of using work-style profiling as a learning tool in the leadership program at the University of Florida. Both sets of research findings demonstrate significant outcomes as a result of using work-style profiling scores to form individualized learning plans. Through analysis of pretest and posttest scores and through follow-up interviews, Salvano found four critical macro themes resulting from participation in the leadership program: (1) subjects demonstrated mastery of their targeted attributes; (2) through committed effort, subjects modified their leadership behaviors and styles; (3) there was an improvement of overall subject talent; and (4) subjects valued interactive educational opportunities, such as participation in conferences or on-the-job mentoring, as their most important learning activity.

One of the most significant findings from the Tunks study (2007) indicated that subjects as a whole demonstrated distinct changes in their data rationale score on the OPQ, an attribute that was identified as critical for college leadership in the Profiles Project (Campbell and Leverty, 1997). During follow-up interviews, Tunks noted that subjects reported mastery of diverse work styles resulting from the learner-centered approach to leadership. Tunks also found that individuals showed significant learning gains related to the attributes they had targeted for improvement on the basis of a program of course work, professional coaching, and individual development.

The focus within the leadership program at the University of Florida enables leaders to make great strides in enhancing their leadership skills. Through the process of personality and work-style profiling and executive coaching in targeted areas of improvement, students become more effective educational leaders.

Consolidating Lessons Learned into Active Interventions

Deutschman (2007) identifies three Rs as the key to enacting change: relate, repeat, and reframe. Deutschman's model has been incorporated into the community college leadership curriculum at the University of Florida.

Relate. The community college leadership program at the University of Florida is structured as a cohort model through which students relate with their peers as they collectively address targeted work styles through group projects. As a cohort, the students engage in peer mentoring and encourage one another to develop the behavioral characteristics needed to become effective leaders. This process is facilitated by department faculty.

Repeat. Through a formative process comprising the OPQ assessment and discussions targeting improvement strategies during scheduled meetings, students repeatedly address their competencies and improvement strategies. This process is tracked through an individualized learning plan that each student co-produces following first administration of the OPQ. Additionally, students are encouraged to participate in conferences and activities such as informational interviews with current leaders in the field. Engaging students in ways that challenge their preferred work styles throughout the program allows them to grow and adopt new modes of working with a variety of situations and tasks.

NEW DIRECTIONS FOR COMMUNITY COLLEGES • DOI: 10.1002/cc

Reframe. Deutschman (2007) describes reframing as a way of changing one's entire outlook on life. Deutschman uses patients with heart disease as his exemplar throughout his work and describes the process of a worldview change from an unhealthy and unhappy existence to one that values personal fulfillment as a result of eating and being healthy, resulting in a substantial lifestyle change. This process is achieved through group support (or relating with peers who understand and support one another's goals) because of being extremely difficult on an individual basis. It represents the successful act of reframing that allows individuals to change.

Through the leadership program at the University of Florida, students are taught to reframe how they approach their work as community college administrators. Through extensive self-study and positive feedback from peers and mentors, students reframe their outlook on college administration. One student entering the program worked as an information technologist and preferred to engage with others through technology modalities. Throughout the program, however, he was challenged to engage in group facilitation and other situations in which he would need to use a work style different from his preference. With ongoing practice through successful learning interventions and executive coaching, this student was able to incorporate new concepts into his thought processes, eventually turning the new style into a natural process. This individual is now the chief academic officer of his college and continuously engages in interpersonal interaction.

Recommendations

The process described here is one that can be implemented as part of any leadership program. Implementing such a program requires a trained faculty member who knows how to interpret assessment data. Students need strong direction and encouragement to facilitate changes. Behavioral change takes time. A minimum of twelve to eighteen months between implementation of pre- and postassessments is recommended.

It is the responsibility of the trained faculty member to initiate periodic assessments and suggest strategies for improvement. Additionally, it is important for program faculty to understand that interpretation of individual scores and implementation of individualized plans for improvement is the preferred method. Group analysis or norm referencing does not promote the desired level of individualized development; an individualized learning plan is assigned to each student in order to help track individual learning outcomes and learning gains.

In addition to a trained faculty mentor, peer mentoring through cohort-based program plans is suggested. Faculty at the University of Florida have identified team-based learning as not only a key pedagogy but also a mastery concept for students to gain as emerging community college leaders. Cross (1998) cites research on cognition and motivation conducted in the field of developmental psychology that can be applied to the benefit of developing leaders. This research states that development of what modern learning theorists call a *schema*, a cognitive map or network that links an individual's own understanding of a concept with that of others toward new understanding of the concept, is essential to students' developmental gains. Cross suggests that peer-oriented learning communities are the key to development of cognitive complexity in students. Developing leaders are especially likely to achieve the greatest learning gains when involvement in peer-relational environments contributes to integration of their experiences. Though the student cited here initially demonstrated difficulty with an approach that necessitated leadership concepts, the holistic benefit of participating in a peer learning environment translated directly into effective leadership in the work environment.

Through learner-centered pedagogical practices in the leadership program, future change leaders are prepared for the challenges they will face throughout their career. Traditional leadership curricula offer exposure to concepts such as trait theory, transformational leadership, situational leadership, and other foundational knowledge bases, which are an important component of leadership development. However, most existing leadership development models do not give students a systematic and sustained mechanism with which to assess development and demonstrate mastery of leadership skills.

Leadership is an inherently self-directed process, but through the interventions discussed in this chapter (such as cohort-based learning, competency assessment and improvement, individualized plans for learning, and use of multiple modes of communication) students can learn to negotiate interpersonal dynamics more effectively. Through implementation of these processes, the gap between traditional leadership development and development of emotionally adept self-aware leaders can be bridged.

Conclusion

Educational leaders have tremendous impact on the field, shaping educational policy and educational practice. They become stewards of the discipline who "have the responsibility to apply knowledge, skills, findings, and insights in the service of problem solving or greater understanding [and] adopting a sense of purpose that is larger than oneself" (Golde, 2007, p. 2). Faculty members at leadership institutes should critically examine and understand the needs of developing leaders to help them make meaning from their own experiences. According to George Boggs, the president of the AACC, future leaders need opportunities to learn, develop, and practice leadership skills through simulations, internships, and mentorships; consequently leadership programs should be structured to provide opportunities for skill development (Boggs, 2003). Placing individualized experiential learning interventions within the context of a social learning environment embodies the progression of educational leadership development called for by Boggs. Through actively incorporating leadership assessment and executive coaching into the curriculum, the University of Florida's leadership development program serves as a mechanism to achieve this ideal.

References

Boggs, G. R. "Leadership Context for the Twenty-First Century." In W. E. Piland and D. B. Wolf (eds.), *Help Wanted: Preparing Community College Leaders in a New Century*. New Directions for Community Colleges, no. 123, pp. 15–25. San Francisco: Jossey-Bass, 2003.

Campbell, D. F. (ed.) *The Leadership Gap: Model Strategies for Leadership Development*. Washington, D.C.: Community College Press, 2002.

Campbell, D. F. "The New Leadership Gap: Shortages in Administrative Positions." *Community College Journal*, 2006, 76(4), 10–14.

Campbell, D. F., and Leverty, L. H. "Developing and Selection of Leaders for the 21st Century." *Community College Journal*, 1997, 67(4), 34–36.

Cross, K. P. "Why Learning Communities? Why Now?" *About Campus*, July–Aug., 1998, 1–11.

Deutschman, A. *Change or Die: The Three Keys to Change at Work and in Life*. New York: HarperCollins, 2007.

Golde, C. M. "Preparing Stewards of the Discipline," 2007. Retrieved Jan. 12, 2009, from http://groups.google.com/group/cped/web/preparing-stewards-of-the-discipline.

Goleman, D. *Working with Emotional Intelligence*. New York: Bantam, 1998.

Salvano, C. R. "Effect of a Community College Leadership Development Program on the Leadership Behaviors of Community College Administrators at a Florida Community College." Unpublished doctoral dissertation, University of Florida, 2005.

Tunks, L. "Comparison of the Outcomes of Leadership Behaviors of Community College Administrators." Unpublished doctoral dissertation, University of Florida, 2007.

DALE F. CAMPBELL is a professor and the director of the Community College Leadership Consortium at the University of Florida.

SYRAJ SYED is a research analyst and Ph.D. candidate in Educational Administration and Policy at the University of Florida.

PHILLIP A. MORRIS is a research fellow and Ph.D. candidate in Higher Education Administration at the University of Florida.

NEW DIRECTIONS FOR COMMUNITY COLLEGES • DOI: 10.1002/cc

Reflection can make community college leaders more effective. Reflection catalysts employed in a leadership development program helped to foster multiple levels of reflection and contributed to the development of participants' reflective dispositions.

Learning to Be Reflective Leaders: A Case Study from the NCCHC Hispanic Leadership Fellows Program

Leila González Sullivan, Colleen Aalsburg Wiessner

In the often frenetic daily activities of community college presidents, there seldom seems to be time to reflect on the events, issues, and challenges that fill each day. Recent research suggests, however, that regular reflection increases leaders' learning and may make them more effective (Densten and Gray, 2001; Stoeckel and Davies, 2007). In the constantly changing environment of today's community college, the practice of reflection may be of great value to new generations of leaders. How, then, do emerging leaders, and even seasoned ones, develop a disposition for and habit of reflection? This chapter suggests ways to do just that.

Emerging leaders of community colleges are very intentional in their preparation for the executive role: completing a doctorate, attending professional development programs, and seeking "stretch" assignments on their campus. Many doctoral programs and training seminars, and some individuals, have adopted the *Leading Forward* competencies developed by the American Association of Community Colleges as a framework for learning to lead (AACC, 2005). These competencies are clustered into six categories: organizational strategies, resource management, communication, collaboration, community college advocacy, and professionalism. Each category includes illustrative skills and behaviors. The last category, professionalism, emphasizes the importance of self-assessment through reflection; lifelong learning; and expressions of values, ethics, and authenticity.

NEW DIRECTIONS FOR COMMUNITY COLLEGES, no. 149, Spring 2010 © 2010 Wiley Periodicals, Inc.
Published online in Wiley InterScience (www.interscience.wiley.com) • DOI: 10.1002/cc.394

In the face of the current retirement tsunami due to aging baby boomers, the community college sector has mounted numerous national, regional, and institutional professional development programs to prepare the next generations of leaders. Most of these efforts are structured to convey needed leadership skills such as those presented in the Leading Forward model, as well as examining the nature of community college challenges and operations. Whatever the framework—competency-based or another model—for preparing community college leaders, with the external environment of community colleges changing constantly, it is not sufficient to simply expand the knowledge base and skills of training participants. It becomes essential to teach them how to *construct* knowledge for themselves based on environmental scanning, experiential learning, and constant reflection on the richness of leadership, as Bolden and Gosling (2006) suggest. Nevertheless, few training programs intentionally incorporate a component for participants to develop habits of reflection. This chapter presents current thinking on the importance of reflective leadership and describes a professional development program for Hispanics who aspire to the community college presidency, a program in which reflection is taught and encouraged as a learning approach. Suggestions for how this approach can be used by individuals, colleges, and training providers are offered at the conclusion of the chapter.

Reflection as a Means for Learning

Schön's 1983 text is commonly identified as the impetus for including reflection as a part of professional practice. It offers two helpful categories: reflection-in-action and reflection-on-action. Potentially, community college leaders engage in reflection both during an experience (in action) and after an experience (on action). The first involves thinking on one's feet; the latter may involve planned and structured reflection activities. These forms of reflection can both be viewed as experiential learning.

Experiential learning is accepted as a primary means for adult learning, and a range of learning experiences, including reflection, are often assigned that label. The relationship between experiential learning and reflection is an important one. As Cell (1984) states, not all experiences result in learning. To learn from experience individuals must reflect on it; without reflection learning may not take place, or the learning may be dysfunctional.

Clearly, more than rational and technical knowledge is needed in the complex areas of practice so common in the daily lives of community college leaders. According to Bateson (1994), survival in a rapidly changing world depends on learning that results in adaptation and improvisation, learning that occurs through reflection on experience. Critical reflection is also important as a means for identifying and questioning assumptions. Thus community college leaders are well advised to develop a disposition toward reflection as a means for constructing needed perspectives from daily experiences in their work context and personal and professional lives. Without reflection, it is easy to repeat past mistakes or fail to repeat approaches that were effective in previous situations. For all of these reasons, reflection is emphasized in the National Community College Hispanic Council Hispanic Leadership Fellows Program.

How Do People Reflect?

For some, reflection is a natural way of being in the world, while others are oblivious to its benefits. Still others may actually resist reflective activities, for a variety of reasons. The value of reflection is endorsed by many, and teaching its value is an important first step. An often-neglected second step is to teach people *how* to reflect. As Chapman and Anderson (2005) note:

> An experienced reflective practitioner establishes a clearly articulated goal for the [reflective practice], makes disciplined use of a personally satisfying method for reflection selected from the many varieties available, regularly assesses what they learn from their reflections, and, above all, makes a commitment to make changes to their practice, personally or professionally, based upon that learning [p. 542].

To foster this level of reflection, Fellows Program participants engage in a range of activities designed to build reflection skills. The program curriculum employs processes the authors developed and named "reflection catalysts," as part of their approach "Learning to Reflect/Reflecting to Learn." Importantly, the Fellows are encouraged to develop a reflective disposition, or, as Willis (1999) writes, to live reflection as a way of being.

Linking Reflection, Leadership Development, and Effective Practice

Stoeckel and Davies (2007) explored how community college presidents experience and use self-reflection in the course of their leadership role. They based their study in the six-stage process of self-reflective learning conceived by Boyd and Fales (1983). These six stages were: "(1) sense of discomfort; (2) identification or clarification of the concern; (3) openness to new information from internal and external sources, with ability to observe and take in from a variety of perspectives; (4) resolution, expressed as 'integration,' 'coming together,' 'acceptance of self-reality,' and 'creative synthesis'; (5) establishing continuity of self with past, present, and future; and (6) deciding whether to act on the outcome of the reflective process" (Boyd and Fales, 1983, p. 106).

Stoeckel and Davies (2007) identified three overarching themes in the data they collected—mindfulness, discovery, and authenticity—as well as several subthemes for each one. The findings were organized according to these themes and were then synthesized into a set of possible applications for community college leaders. These researchers concluded that the presidents in the study built their own personalized approach to self-reflection and consciously and regularly made time for this activity. Further, the presidents engaged others in the reflective process and fostered a campus culture that supported reflection. Finally, these leaders continuously clarified their own values, made time for self-care, and above all used self-reflection as a means of being authentic. For the purposes of fostering self-reflection among the Hispanic Fellows and assessing the learning that took place in the professional development program, the program planners adopted Stoeckel and Davies's themes, which will be discussed in more detail later in this chapter.

Densten and Gray (2001) examined the connection between leadership development and reflection, grounding their discussion in Dewey's definition of reflective thinking: "Active, persistent, and careful consideration of any belief or supposed form of knowledge in the light of the grounds that support it and the further conclusions to which it tends, constitutes reflective thought" (1933, p. 6). Further, Densten and Gray noted that those who use critical reflection for learning generally have three attributes: open-mindedness to alternative views, responsibility through an active search for truth, and wholeheartedness in their dedication to reflective processes. In contrast, the writers asserted, the unreflective leader might experience serious negative consequences as a result of not understanding how a leader's use of power affects others, not questioning the consequences of one's actions, not challenging one's favorable perceptions of self, and not seeing situations from multiple perspectives. Practice in reflective techniques, then, is an important component of any leadership program so that emerging leaders adopt a lifelong habit of and disposition toward reflection.

The NCCHC Hispanic Leadership Fellows Program

The Hispanic Leadership Fellows Program is sponsored by the National Community College Hispanic Council, an affiliate of the American Association of Community Colleges, to prepare Hispanic community college administrators for executive leadership positions including the presidency. It operates under the joint sponsorship of NCCHC and North Carolina State University. Training components include two intensive seminars, skills assessment, cross-cultural discussions, mentoring by Hispanic presidents, case studies, career planning, and networking. The program planners seek to develop reflective habits in the participants, urging them to act as ethical individuals *and* reflective leaders, which is the more public role that they play. They are encouraged to make reflection part of their leadership style and become role models in these habits so that others will be inspired to develop reflective practices as well. In this way, whole organizations will adopt a reflective culture.

New Learning data forms were used in the program to elicit from participants *what* (content) they had learned and *how* (process) they had learned it. Qualitative analysis of these data forms indicated that during the training seminars the Fellows constructed new knowledge about leadership, the community college presidency, the community of practice (Hispanic presidents) into which they were being invited, and themselves as leaders. They also exhibited the intention to apply their learning in current and future jobs and were better able to picture themselves in the presidency (Haley, Wiessner, and Robinson, 2009; Wiessner and Sullivan, 2007).

To explore more deeply the role of reflection in learning and knowledge construction, the 2007 cohort of Fellows was asked to participate in guided reflections as well as recording their thoughts on New Learning data forms. A series of reflection catalysts (guided activities) was developed for use at particular points in the professional development event; these contained specific reflection prompts aligned with program goals. During the planning stage, the researchers discussed the potential benefits of using only the reflection catalysts but chose to pursue a two-pronged approach, determining that the general reflections on New Learning forms helped to develop reflection as a habit that occurs in ongoing ways and not just when prompted by a specific request or an attractive reflection catalyst.

An additional cycle of reflection involved the researchers' mirroring back through New Learning reports to the group their reflections in a way that allowed them to see what they and others had learned. The New Learning reports took a variety of creative art forms to stimulate right-brained thinking and help participants view their experiences and their learning from different perspectives.

Evidence of the Beginnings of Reflective Disposition

An important point in participants' professional development occurred when they began to make reflective statements related to their future role as leader. One cohort member said, "I feel energized and inspired. Today I feel like I am looking at the face of the future in terms of Leadership at Community Colleges. This is the training ground for tomorrow's leaders!" Or, as another remarked, "It's not a matter of IF . . . It's a matter of when."

The authors sought to determine if the Fellows demonstrated Stoeckel and Davies's categories of reflective leadership (mindfulness, discovery, and authenticity; 2007) as described earlier. Multiple examples of each habit of reflection were found in the participants' written statements and are included in the samples here. Using this schema, it became clear that there was a progression or deepening in the participants' reflections from the June to the September training sessions. Yet, as expected, the closer the reflection was to Stoeckel and Davies' category of authenticity, the fewer the number of statements submitted. Also, with the addition of more specific reflective activities, this current cohort illustrated an overall progression toward deeper and multileveled reflection.

The first four habits of reflection relate to *mindfulness*. The first, *internal environment*, focused on and about self. One participant noted that "there is so much to learn and experience on the road to becoming a college president." Another questioned, "But just because we can do it and we will be good at it, and we are trained for it . . . should we? Is it the right thing for me and for the life I want to lead?"

In the second habit related to mindfulness, *external environment*, the Fellows exhibited attention to surroundings. One focused on the importance of a leader's awareness: "Just small things can have big effects—big things can happen in a short amount of time." Another reflected on his or her connection to the external environment of the community college context: "I wonder what opportunities I will now have as a result of my participation in the fellows program. Will others at my college/district truly hold my experience in such high regard as me?" A third remarked, "I wonder how we will do as the new leaders of NCCHC."

When their mindfulness was focused on the third habit, *people*, the Fellows reflected on relationships. They focused on connections in the cohort in statements such as, "One of the things I always look forward to is the 'group bonding.' I feel the undercurrents of the group are very, very positive—one of my favorite experiences ever." They also referred to relationships important to leadership: "I have come to realize that an individual cannot perform by him or herself. It takes a team . . . to get to where an institution needs to be." Or, "This picture represents the need for a strong and diverse leadership team. The presidency is too much for any one person. You will need to develop a bond made of trust in order to make it work. Seeing all the hands centered as they are tells me that we are all in this together."

The fourth habit related to mindfulness, *Socratic dialogue,* involved questioning, examining self, and searching for inner truths, as evidenced in these statements: "I often feel that I am the one in the meeting who sees things that others don't or that I can see the next step when others are searching. I think it is 'intuitively obvious' . . . [this] is *my* strength area." In response to an activity related to change, another reasoned, "My college is going through a tremendous change right now. I see systems and see the new culture we seek. I feel confined by not being able to communicate this. Perhaps everyone has different bricks and can't visualize A to B."

Discovery includes three habits of reflection: *origins and values, personal growth through learning,* and *vulnerability and struggles.* In reflecting on origins and values, the Fellows looked at their background, experiences, and values formation. One wrote about culture:

> I can honestly say I never considered how my culture impacts my leadership style and development. As I begin to refine my leadership skill in preparation to become a president, I think it's important for me to reflect on

the cultural influences regarding my leadership style and how that impacts other cultures within an organization. I seriously never considered this!

Another reflected, "Education is a bonding element no matter at what level or institution you come from. Education is a common thread that opens the door for dialogue."

Their reflections on personal growth through learning were evident in these statements: "As a result of my experience in the Fellows Program, I now believe more firmly that it is critical to be cognizant of one's limitations in approaching the discussion to become an executive leader (CEO, VP, etc.)." Or, "I see a bright future ahead because of those that have come before me. The only difference is that I am now more aware and more focused because of the fellows program and the people that have committed to our success." Another stated, "I am immensely grateful (exhausted, too) for having fate and determination get me to this place called the NCCHC Fellows Program. I don't know what the future holds, but there are so many experiences I can draw on."

They also recognized and owned their vulnerability and struggles. "Rosecolored [sic] glasses—you can't hide behind them with idealism. Reality is here, the choice is ours." Or, "Many Latino presidents have had many barriers to overcome. We can all relate to one another." Yet another stated, "You have to take a broad view and perspective and not be narrowly focused because you never know what is around the corner . . . because of the vantage point you can see the dangers, rocks and barriers that you otherwise would not see."

The final category, *authenticity*, involves two habits of reflection: *striving for congruence* and *expressions of authenticity*. Striving for congruence involves reflecting on self and values, as expressed by another participant who acknowledged that "I have to take care of myself, my health. Family is important." And, "The presidency is reached through many paths. It is important to find balance between the professional and personal life."

Expressions of authenticity involve taking action based on understanding of self and values, risk taking, self-care, continuous clarification of values, continuous learning, and creating an environment for reflection. For example, "I'm getting to know myself better on different levels. This is a good beginning. Need to follow up when I get home to close the gap." Another participant embodied authenticity in this way while viewing a photo as a catalyst for reflection:

> The reason I chose this picture is that it reflects my major theme during the past few years: transformation. I think about transformation for myself, because this is the first time in my life where I have given myself a breather to reflect on who I am and what I want. . . . What I liked about the photo was that transformation involves movement, jumping, becoming airborne for a while, and it usually involves the support, anchoring and lift from another person.

There is no question that the program's reflective activities added a level of engagement that participants did not always welcome during long days of work. Nevertheless, eventually they did embrace its value, and their learning is evident. They accepted it as a dimension of the program and even began to anticipate it. Through their experiences of reflection the Fellows did begin to see ways that reflective activities could be integrated in their work back home on an ongoing basis.

Implications for Practice in the Community College Context

On the basis of theoretical perspectives gleaned from the literature and experience with the Hispanic Leadership Fellows Program, the authors propose a number of suggestions for developing a disposition toward reflection at the individual and institutional level, as well as in programs designed to prepare new change leaders.

Individuals

- Make and carry out a firm commitment to regular reflection.
- Understand your reflective style and find reflective tools that dovetail with that style.
- Intentionally and regularly set aside time without interruption in a setting that relaxes and fosters deep, free thought.
- Use visualization techniques to explore ideas and possibilities; imagine a photograph of "my day" and examine the details of the picture.
- Tell a story; unexpected details often surface as the story unfolds and these can lead to further reflection and understanding.
- Look away or look elsewhere; rather than focusing directly on an object or incident, allow thoughts to drift or wander, with the possibility that unanticipated ideas and connections will emerge.
- Try to capture random images and thoughts during regular activities that suggest areas for reflection.

Institutions

- Take time for intentional reflection in meetings; allow silent time for attendees to think, make associations, collect impressions.
- Use metaphors that encourage distinctive thinking about a situation, event, or outlook.
- Encourage unexpected connections, divergent thinking, expressions of values.
- Avoid judgments of ideas that emerge from reflection; incorporate the ideas as ways to extend and broaden thinking in groups.
- Use debriefings as a form of reflection.
- Use such reflective activities judiciously; don't overdo.

NEW DIRECTIONS FOR COMMUNITY COLLEGES • DOI: 10.1002/cc

Leadership program providers, including graduate programs

- Build reflection into the program intentionally in nonintrusive ways.
- Use a variety of techniques to stimulate reflection, including metaphors, visuals, quiet time, and free writing.
- Encourage narratives, sharing of experiences and values, and self-questioning to explore behaviors and decisions.
- Encourage knowledge co-construction, asking participants/students to consider each other's ideas and build on them; take note of new knowledge that emerges from this spiraling process.
- Emphasize the importance of reflection to effective performance and authenticity and the need to create a lifelong disposition toward reflection.

Conclusion

Reflecting on the experience of incorporating a reflection component in the Hispanic Leadership Fellows Program, the authors have come to a deeper understanding of its importance and value for community college leaders and those who aspire to a leadership role in a context of change. Reflection seems to be a natural process for some, while for others it must be learned and practiced. It may begin as an apparently extraneous activity, almost artificial, but needs eventually to become internal, a continuous process, a lifelong disposition, and a consciously applied means for greater effectiveness in leadership. Reflection can be hard work, extra work, but its benefits are immeasurable in both personal and institutional terms.

References

American Association of Community Colleges. *Leading Forward Competencies for Community College Leaders*. Washington, D.C.: AACC, 2005.
Bateson, M. C. *Peripheral Visions: Learning Along the Way*. New York: HarperCollins, 1994.
Bolden, R., and Gosling, J. "Leadership Competencies: Time to Change the Tune?" *Leadership*, 2006, 2(2), 147–163.
Boyd, E. M., and Fales, A. W. "Reflective Learning: Key to Learning from Experience." *Journal of Humanistic Psychology*, 1983, 23(2), 99–117.
Cell, E. *Learning to Learn from Experience*. Albany: State University of New York Press, 1984.
Chapman, V. L., and Anderson, B. S. "Reflective Practice." In L. M. English (ed.), *International Encyclopedia of Adult Education*. New York: Palgrave Macmillan, 2005.
Densten, I. L., and Gray, J. H. "Leadership Development and Reflection: What Is the Connection?" *International Journal of Educational Management*, 2001, 15(3), 119–124.
Dewey, J. *How We Think*. Boston: Heath, 1933.
Haley, K. J., Wiessner, C. A., and Robinson, E. E. "Encountering New Information and Perspectives: Constructing Knowledge in Conference Contexts." *Journal of Continuing Higher Education*, 2009, 53(2), 72–82.
Schön, D. A. *The Reflective Practitioner: How Professionals Think in Action*. New York: Basic Books, 1983.
Stoeckel, P. R., and Davies, T. G. "Reflective Leadership by Selected Community College Presidents." *Community College Journal of Research and Practice*, 2007, 31(11), 895–912.

Wiessner, C. A., and Sullivan, L. G. "New Learning: Constructing Knowledge in Leadership Training Programs." *Community College Review*, 2007, *35*(2), 88–112.

Willis, P. "Looking for What It's Really Like: Phenomenology in Reflective Practice." *Studies in Continuing Education*, 1999, *21*(1), 91–101.

LEILA GONZÁLEZ SULLIVAN *is the W. Dallas Herring Professor of Community College Education at North Carolina State University.*

COLLEEN AALSBURG WIESSNER *was an assistant professor of adult education at North Carolina State University. The theory of transformative learning in training and conference settings that she was building at the time of her death is her legacy, together with her colorful vision of the world and constant support for her students.*

This chapter describes major factors influencing the shape, content, and direction of the new EdD programs and discusses some unique challenges in establishing a separate cohort program in community college leadership. These insights may be useful as individuals examine graduate programs in leadership development, and as community college search committees seek to hire new leaders.

6

University-Based Community College Leadership Programs: Where Future Community College Leaders Are Prepared

Janice Nahra Friedel

Community college leadership programs may take a variety of forms, among them university-based programs, leadership institutes, community college-based "grow your own" programs, professional organization-based institutes, or a combination of these. University-based doctorate leadership programs are the principal providers of these leaders. Seventy percent of community college presidents have a doctorate degree in education (Wallin, Sullivan, and McDade, 2009). In 2006, the California legislature took action to avoid an educational leadership crisis predicted because of a large number of school and community college leaders retiring, increased student populations, and an insufficient pool or pipeline of qualified applicants. Senate Bill 724 amended California's Master Plan for Higher Education to authorize the California State University to award the doctorate in educational administration and leadership for K–12 schools, and community colleges and postsecondary education. The EdD is to be designed for completion in three years (including the dissertation) by full-time working educational personnel. This chapter discusses some of the issues and considerations as a university develops and builds the institutional, departmental, and program infrastructure to support its first doctorate program, the EdD with a separate cohort for community college leadership. These issues are complex

and most often off the radar of the community college practitioner. Implications for practice and the future are proposed.

Call for Reform of Doctorate Education

The need for a new generation of community college leaders converges with a number of factors affecting the design and substance of doctoral leadership programs, including the major trends having an impact on community colleges (such as the stresses of an increasing student population with greater diversity, higher accountability, and the challenges of aligning curriculum throughout the K–16 continuum), regional accreditation standards, and the Carnegie Foundation's call for reform of doctorate education.

Over the last decades, criticism of doctoral education in the United States has continued to mount. The critics cite underrepresentation of women and ethnic minorities, a high student attrition rate exceeding 50 percent in some departments, and doctorate award recipients "ill-prepared to function effectively in their work settings" (Golde and Walker, 2006, p. 5).

Lee Shulman, president of the Carnegie Foundation, articulates a clear purpose of doctoral education: development of students as "stewards of the discipline," individuals who can generate new knowledge, critically conserve valuable and useful knowledge and ideas, and responsibly transform knowledge through writing, publication, teaching, and application. Stewardship connotes ethical and moral dimensions (Golde and Walker, 2006).

In 2001, the Carnegie Foundation began its five-year project, the Carnegie Initiative on the Doctorate (CID), to engage the collegiate community in critical reflection and deliberation in examining doctoral education and to develop creative solutions and approaches to increase their effectiveness. The project focused its work in six disciplines: chemistry, education, English, history, mathematics, and neuroscience.

The CID called for retooling of the EdD.

> Most students in Ed.D. programs do not aim to be researchers, though their doctoral programs often treat them as such by offering experiences more similar to Ph.D. programs than to the high-level preparation for practice or leadership. . . . Too often, the Ed.D. is defined by subtraction, with fewer requirements than the Ph.D. . . . Instead of being valued for accomplishing the discrete ends it was originally designed for, the Ed.D. is widely regarded as a "Ph.D. Lite" . . . [Shulman] cautions that unless we face these issues squarely and with purposeful action, schools of education risk becoming increasingly impotent in carrying out their primary missions—the advancement of knowledge and the preparation of quality practitioners [Shulman, Golde, Bueschel, and Garabedian, 2006, p. 25].

Shulman et al. suggest we must "move forward on two fronts: rethinking and reclaiming the research doctorate (the Ph.D.) with its strong links to practice, and developing a robust and distinct professional practice doctor-ate (the P.P.D.)" (2006, p. 27), whether we call it an EdD or decide to use another name. In the context of the professional practice doctorate, Shulman speaks of "stewards of the practice" and the attributes of the leaders we pre-pare. He summarizes these attributes as the six domains of professional prac-tice stewardship: service, understanding, technique, judgment, action, and engagement in professional communities (Shulman and Golde, 2008).

The CID concludes that "the quality of interaction between teacher and learner matters at least as much as the formal design and requirements of the program" (Walker, Golde, Jones, Bueschel, and Hutchings, 2008, p. 85). The report suggests a number of activities universities can undertake to engage students and faculty in intellectual community (pp. 127–133):

- Engaging students fully in the life of the department
- Collaborative work on curriculum
- Sharing research across boundaries
- Opening classroom doors
- Allowing risk and failure
- Setting aside time for reflection
- Creating physical spaces for intellectual community
- Social events

Some of the suggestions may prove challenging for EdD programs designed for delivery to a cohort comprising full-time employed commu-nity college personnel.

In March 2007, the Carnegie Foundation and the Council of Academic Deans for Research Education Institutions (CADREI) launched the Carnegie Project on the Education Doctorate (CPED), a three-year effort to "reclaim the education doctorate and to transform it into a degree of choice for the next generation of school and college leaders." Its goal is to "strengthen every facet of the program" (Carnegie Foundation, CPED, n.d.). At the June 2008 Convening of the Carnegie Project on the Education Doctorate, it was stated that:

> The Ed.D. . . . is critical for the practical improvement and reform of educa-tion . . . in the generation of new teachers . . . [and in] providing needed lead-ership for the most rapidly growing segment of the American higher education system, which is the community colleges. The coming eight years . . . look like the perfect time to emphasize these kinds of activities. Doctoral education has always been dominated by a view of asking questions that are timeless, rather than timely, broad and overarching. And that is fine. That is what Ph.D.s are all about. They are about the human legacy but they aren't necessarily the best way to prepare the best and brightest leaders and educa-tors. And that is why it's terribly important to do this now [Shulman and Golde, 2008].

New Directions for Community Colleges • DOI: 10.1002/cc

The California State University Experience

The California State University (CSU), with its twenty-three campuses, enrolls more than 450,000 students annually. As it embarked on development and establishment of the EdD, each campus conducted assessments to determine both supply and demand for new educational leaders in K–12 schools and districts, and in community colleges. The advisory committee for California State University Northridge's (CSUN) EdD program recommended separate cohorts for K–12 and for community college leadership.

Only one-third of students starting a doctorate in education have an undergraduate degree in education (Golde and Walker, 2006); the pipeline of community college doctoral students typically begins in the academic disciplines, general administration, and other functional units of the college. There can be no assumption that doctoral students have a common core of understanding regarding the comprehensive community college, its organization, and its administration and management. Their diverse backgrounds can both enrich the learning process and challenge the program and faculty. Indeed, the success of the program may be dependent on the diversity of the experiences the students bring to it.

One of the most basic elements in designing an education doctorate program is the students and their characteristics, goals, and passions. Certainly students need strong conceptual, analytical, and writing skills to ensure their readiness for the rigors of the program. Students may represent a cross-section of the community college: academic disciplines, student services, finance, administration, physical plant, instructional and information technologies, noncredit and continuing education, workforce, economic development. With such diverse and specialized professional backgrounds, the doctorate program faculty may be intimidated by individual student expertise or challenged by a lack of basic core knowledge regarding the comprehensive nature of community colleges and their administration. Additionally, some students may not yet aspire to the presidency but want to take incremental steps in community college leadership. A program would need to provide relevance and rigor to those aspiring to midlevel administrative and leadership positions as well as to those seeking a presidency.

Student Learning Outcomes

A set of student learning outcomes (SLOs) for the doctoral program, common to both the K–12 and the community college cohorts, incorporates and builds on the American Association of Community Colleges (AACC) Competencies for Community College Leaders, the California Professional Standards for Educational Leaders (CPSELS), and the national Interstate Schools Leaders Licensure Consortium Standards (ISLLC). These SLOs are broader than the AACC competencies and incorporate the dispositions of the doctoral program candidates. The candidates for the CSUN doctorate in educational leadership will have the knowledge, skills, and disposition to lead profound change in teaching and learning in K–14 institutions by:

1. Planning systemic reform and managing the change process in collaboration with fellow educators and other stakeholders, on the basis of a shared vision of learning
2. Guiding and supporting staff in nurturing a school, district, or community college culture and program conducive to effective instruction of all students and to the professional growth of all employees
3. Using data and technology effectively to assess student achievement, evaluate staff and programs, and plan and implement accountability systems
4. Becoming critical consumers of educational research and producers of action research who apply the lessons of research to student, school or district, or community college improvement
5. Promoting culturally proficient policies and practices that recognize and value difference and ensure equity
6. Managing fiscal, physical, and human resources to ensure an effective, safe learning and working environment
7. Collaborating with families and community members, responding to diverse community interests and needs, and mobilizing community resources at the local, state, and federal levels
8. Modeling ethical practice, strong skills in communication and collaboration, and development of leadership capacity in oneself and others
9. Understanding, navigating, responding to, and influencing the larger policy environment (CSUN Doctoral Candidate Handbook, 2008, pp. 3–4)

CSUN Program Development

Numerous program details had to be developed and issues resolved, including multiple reviews and approvals. The program and course proposals were submitted to the appropriate university curriculum committees and granted approval. A central program feature is customization of the curriculum for the community college cohort. Differentiation of the curriculum for the K–12 and the community college cohorts is most evident in the courses: Postsecondary Finance and Enrollment Management, Law and Policy in Postsecondary Education, Instructional Assessment and Program Evaluation, Entrepreneurship in the Community College, and Human Resources Management. An application to the Structural Change Panel of the Western Association of Schools and Colleges (WASC) Accrediting Commission for Senior Colleges and Universities to offer a doctoral degree in EdD with emphases in K–12 and community college education was submitted and approved. The WASC application stressed establishment and nurturance of a doctoral-level culture.

According to WASC, the "doctoral culture" is evidenced by the (1) elements of doctoral level course requirements; (2) nature of the research environment; (3) balance between applied and research components of the degree; (4) type of culminating experience (full dissertation or a culminating/capstone project); (5) plans for faculty research; (6) library resources; (7) peer and campus collaboration; (8) how students (full- and part-time) will be integrated into the intellectual community of the department and institution; and (9) student assessment, and qualifying examination for candidacy.

At CSUN, multiple considerations in development and implementation of its first doctorate program and nurturance of a doctoral culture would be the catalyst for departmental and institutional transformation and a continuous cycle of reexamination and reflection. The national discourse regarding transformation of the doctorate, and specifically the education doctorate, centers around the question of purpose. So too did the discussion at CSUN. The goal of CSUN's EdD was determined to be preparation of competent and reflective leaders committed to moral and ethical actions and capable of serving as change agents and solving problems in complex organizations.

Numerous operational issues had to be resolved as the program was being developed and implemented. Among them were governance of the program; program directorship; recruitment and hiring of faculty, especially community college leaders who are scholar-practitioners; and finding the institutional resources to develop and begin program implementation. Development of the EdD did not receive a state appropriation, so its initial operational costs would have to be accommodated through reallocation of university resources. Other issues included sustaining the engagement of an advisory committee, informing community college faculty and administrators about the program and building credibility and confidence in the new program, identifying and engaging mentors for the doctoral students, and maintaining an appropriate balance between research and theory.

As CSUN embarks on enrollment of its first community college doctoral program cohort, questions and issues continue:

- How do you create, nurture, and sustain a doctoral culture among faculty and students?
- How does the institution support the research of faculty and students?
- How does the university create and foster an intellectual community of students and faculty?
- What is the role of the advisor and the dissertation chair?
- What are the research expectations for community college leaders, and how is this knowledge used to determine the scope and depth of the research methodology courses?
- How do you assess the preparedness of doctoral students to engage in meaningful research? To what depth do the students need to understand and be able to conduct quantitative and qualitative analysis? Would a pre-program, boot-camp-style research methodology or statistics course be necessary?
- How does the program attract and retain both core and affiliate faculty?

NEW DIRECTIONS FOR COMMUNITY COLLEGES • DOI: 10.1002/cc

- What are the incentives for faculty to serve as dissertation committee chair and to serve on a dissertation committee?
- How does the university attract faculty members who are successful community college leaders and are also scholar-practitioners (that is, they have a record of research and scholarship)?
- How does faculty salary compete with the salary paid to community college administrators?
- How can a program afford to bring new faculty on board for program and curriculum development, without students enrolled in the program yet? How are faculty load issues resolved during the initial years of the program offering?
- How do you create a culture of evidence and inquiry for an EdD in community college leadership? What will be the indicators of success?
- How do you meaningfully engage students in developing the evaluation process for the program and in refinement of the curriculum?

Development of the EdD is an ongoing process of review, reflection, and renewal. New faculty with community college experience were hired in August 2008 to assist in customizing the curriculum for the community college cohort, to participate in program refinement and professional development, to transition from the field to the academy, and to network with the faculty, administrators and staff at the regional community colleges. Informational sessions at regional community college locations were conducted by the new doctoral faculty to build awareness about the program and its practitioner orientation. The first EdD cohort in K–12 leadership began in fall 2008; the first community college cohort began in fall 2009.

The Future and Implications for Practice

Initiation of the CSUN's EdD coincides with one of the most challenging fiscal times facing California and its educational institutions. A key question is the capacity of the Los Angeles and San Fernando Valley regions to sustain two separate cohorts. The ability of CSUN to balance the multiple drivers on the design of its program with the needs and interests of its students and its regional educational institutions will determine its future success.

Another key question centers around how realistic it is to expect students to complete the education doctorate in three years when the "average 'registered time-to-degree' for education doctorates is 8.3 years" (Golde and Walker, 2006, p. 246).

As the new EdD program is established and implemented, CSUN's separate cohort programs will be monitored and evaluated; short-term and long-term measures of success will be refined and used to evaluate the effectiveness of the program in increasing student achievement and success. CSUN's EdD program, with its blend of theory and practice and its signature pedagogy of case study and problem-based inquiry, was developed within the context of the Carnegie Foundation's focus on the education doctorate and the call to create stewards of the practice. Colleges and universities seeking to establish EdD programs in community college leadership may learn from the efforts of CSUN.

Establishment of CSUN's community college cohort doctoral program is a demonstration of the maturity of the university's relationship with its regional community colleges. The relationships forged and enhanced through establishment of the doctoral program have the potential to evolve into dynamic partnerships where the higher education community comes together around a common set of goals related to systemic K–16 educational reform and student achievement and success.

References

California State University Northridge. *CSUN Doctoral Candidate Handbook*. Northridge: CSUN, 2008.

Carnegie Foundation for the Advancement of Education. "Carnegie Project on the Education Doctorate." Retrieved Apr. 5, 2009, from http://www.carnegiefoundation.org/general/index.asp?key=1867.

Golde, C., and Walker, G. (eds.). *Envisioning the Future of Doctorate Education: Preparing Stewards of the Discipline*. (Carnegie Essays on the Doctorate.) San Francisco: Jossey-Bass, 2006.

Shulman, L. and Golde, C. "Envisioning Stewards: Dialogue with Lee Schulman and Chris Golde." June 2008 Convening of the Carnegie Project on the Education Doctorate (CPED), 2008. Retrieved Apr. 14, 2009, from http://video.google.com/videoplay?docid=5833334653819204634.

Schulman, L. S., Golde, C. M., Bueschel, A. C., & Garabedian, K. J. "Reclaiming Education's Doctorates: A Critique and a Proposal." *Educational Researcher*, 2006, 35(3), 25–32.

Walker, G. E., Golde, C. M., Jones L., Bueschel, A. C., and Hutchings, P. *The Formation of Scholars: Rethinking Doctoral Education for the Twenty-First Century*. San Francisco: Jossey-Bass, 2008.

Wallin, D., Sullivan, L. G., and McDade, S. Priming the Pump: Preparing the Leadership Pipeline Through Targeted Leadership Development Programs. Session presented at 2009 American Association of Community Colleges Annual Conference, Phoenix, Ariz., April 2009.

JANICE NAHRA FRIEDEL is professor, educational leadership and policy studies, California State University Northridge (CSUN).

This chapter describes a multitude of leadership programs designed to provide administrators serving in the middle part of the organization with opportunities for new skill development and enhancement of existing skills.

Leading from the Middle: Preparing Leaders for New Roles

Larry Ebbers, Kitty S. Conover, Anisha Samuels

The graying of community college leadership is on the rise and well documented. Many community college presidents, upper-level administrators, and experienced faculty who began their careers in the sixties, seventies, and even eighties are nearing the end of their career, leaving key leadership openings to be filled (Duree, 2007; Shults, 2001). The average age of sitting community college presidents is fifty-eight, and nearly 84 percent of current community college presidents will retire by 2016 (Weisman and Vaughan, 2007). Further, presidents report that 38 percent of their chief administrators will retire by 2016 (Weisman and Vaughan, 2007).

One problem community colleges face is the difficulty in finding and identifying new, fully qualified leaders ready to replace those retiring: "Leadership in the community college has suffered from benign neglect. There is little conscious attention paid to questions of where community college leaders will come from, how their talents will be developed, and their experience valued" (Community College Leadership Development Initiative, 2000; McFarlin, Crittenden, and Ebbers, 1997). This problem is precipitated by the lack of future leaders in the community college pipeline. Existing leaders must start identifying, training, and "growing their own" to meet the increasing need for new leadership. A typical career pathway to a senior-level or executive-level position begins with aspiring leaders in the middle (Amey and VanDerLinden, 2002). Succession planning will become critical in the next decade. Part of the process necessitates creation of programs that will help develop future leaders.

NEW DIRECTIONS FOR COMMUNITY COLLEGES, no. 149, Spring 2010 © 2010 Wiley Periodicals, Inc.
Published online in Wiley InterScience (www.interscience.wiley.com) • DOI: 10.1002/cc.396

To fill the growing vacancies, Grow Your Own Leaders (GYOL) programs, as well as statewide and national leadership development programs, present an opportunity for middle managers to begin planning for their own future. The American Association of Community Colleges (AACC) has provided guidelines for middle managers to develop their expertise. Programs have been developed by AACC to assist in development of future leaders. A project funded by the W. K. Kellogg Foundation has led to additional attention to leadership development programs. The project, Leading Forward, outlines recommendations and leadership competencies to enhance leadership development in community colleges (AACC, 2005). With a focus on new leaders, this initiative is offering insight regarding how colleges can cultivate new leadership and foster the needed skill sets for future leaders.

Leadership programs come in many forms. An excellent example of a successful program at the national level is the Future Leaders Institute, organized and promoted by the AACC. These seminars are designed for midlevel community college administrators ready to move to a higher level of leadership. An advanced FLI seminar is offered for those seeking a presidency. Other national programs designed for senior-level aspirants are the Executive Leadership Institute (ELI), sponsored by the League for Innovation, the American Association of Community College Trustees President Preparation workshops (ACCT), and the Chair Academy based at Maricopa Community College in Arizona.

Many states have followed the Grow Your Own Leaders program by instituting statewide programs for middle and upper-level managers. Among them are Iowa, Illinois, Massachusetts, Kentucky, and Louisiana, and others are in various forms of development (Hull and Kiem, 2007; Jeandron, 2006). In addition, some community colleges have developed their own GYOL programs, notably Central Piedmont College in North Carolina, the Community College of Philadelphia, Metropolitan Community College in Nebraska, Johnson County Community College in Kansas, and others. These colleges tend to be large institutions with strong staff development resources; while they are important for institutional GYOLs programs, most smaller institutions have to depend on statewide programs for leader development (Jeandron, 2006).

Stepping Stones for Middle Managers

A plethora of programs for leadership development exist, but those professionals in the middle must also accept responsibility for their own development. To fill the pipeline, the authors suggest development of Stepping Stones for Middle Managers. Because nearly 90 percent of future community college leaders will come from within (McFarlin, Crittenden, and Ebbers, 1997) it is imperative that some steps be taken for aspiring administrators. The proposed stepping stones are engaging, planning, credentialing, and emulating.

NEW DIRECTIONS FOR COMMUNITY COLLEGES • DOI: 10.1002/cc

Engaging. Individuals considering an upper-level management position must make the decision to move up through a personal and professional process. Although the two are intertwined, it is helpful to begin with a variety of personal assessments to help understand the personal and professional attributes of the individual. Aspiring leaders should be aware of their own personality as well as others' so they can interact effectively and solve problems within a variety of professional settings.

Many institutions offer career and personal development activities as in-service programs. Some assessments (inventories) that include personality and leadership types are the DiSC, the Myers Briggs Type Indicator (MBTI), the True Colors Personality Assessment, and StrengthsFinder. Another assessment may include emotional intelligence, commonly referred to as EQ, which might be more important than IQ. In "Working with Emotional Intelligence" (1998), Daniel Goleman states: "Our emotional intelligence determines our potential for learning the practical skills that are based on its five elements: self-awareness, motivation, self-regulation, empathy, and adeptness in relationships. Our emotional competence, on the other hand, shows how much of that potential we have translated into on-the-job capabilities" (p. 3).

Planning. On the basis of engagement and the commitment toward advancing to upper-level administration, each individual needs to develop a personal plan of action. The plan should be designed with flexibility and include goals, timelines, and personal and professional activities. These plans should include (1) completion of degrees appropriate for the position before assuming leadership, (2) involvement with leadership programs outside formal education, and (3) participation in activities specifically targeting the competencies recommended by AACC (Duree, 2007). These competencies include organizational strategy, resource management, communication, collaboration, community college advocacy, and professionalism (AACC, 2005).

Credentialing. Regardless of the position desired, one of the most important aspects of job attainment is an appropriate degree from an accredited institution. With the advent of new delivery systems, degrees are attainable in a variety of formats and learning environments. Future leaders must seek out programs that fit their needs. AACC maintains a list of programs that prepare community college leaders at the master's and doctoral levels on their Web site. Degrees outside of education also offer appropriate credentials: doctoral programs for a respective discipline, a J.D., or an M.B.A. Without the appropriate credential, an applicant will likely be screened out of the process for a position that would have been a logical move in a career path. It is evident that if the goal is to be at the senior executive level in a community college the doctorate degree is fast becoming a prerequisite.

Certificate programs offered by many colleges and universities and professional associations offer specifically targeted areas of study that can enhance one's development in areas such as business and finance, fundraising, and marketing and communications. McFarlin, Crittenden, and Ebbers

(1997) found that those presidents who study in focused community college leadership academic programs are more likely to be highly recognized leaders (McFarlin, Crittenden, and Ebbers, 1997).

Emulating. This is a process of watching and learning from successful experienced leaders. It includes two key concepts: mentoring and networking. The concept most often talked about is finding a mentor. Amey and VanDerLinden (2002) describe mentor–protégé relationships as being long and professionally centered relationships in which an aspiring leader is provided career and encouragement by an experienced leader. In their study of community college leaders, more than 56 percent of the respondents had been in a mentor-protégé relationship. Additionally, 42 percent had been mentors for someone else and 18 percent had mentored more than one person. In his study of community college presidents, Duree (2007) reported that about half of the presidents indicated they had a mentor at some time during their career.

McDade (2005) studied community college presidents and their protégés. The process of helping develop future leaders was thought by those exemplary presidents to be a professional obligation. Boggs (2003) posited that future community college leaders will be selected or hired for their demonstrated knowledge and skills; they will need opportunities to learn to develop and practice these skills through simulations, internships, and mentorships.

If colleges offered individuals interested in leadership intentional development activities or cross-functional training, these activities could help prepare aspiring change leaders for their role. Experiences that allow them an opportunity to practice leadership skills would enable the new leaders to assume a position with greater ease and perhaps make advancement more attractive (Garza Mitchell and Eddy, 2008).

Networking and Succession Planning

Networking is very important inasmuch as the community college world is small, in the sense of people knowing and working with each other. As a part of the mentor-protégé relationship, individuals should look for mentors to help them develop networking skills. Current community college presidents are demonstrating a growing commitment to leadership development through identification of potential leaders, support of in-house leadership programs such as GYOL, and mentor-protégé relationships (Duree, 2007). Completing these stepping stones will assist in planning and assessing the next career step. According to the survey results conducted by Duree: "Approximately one out of two current community college leaders participated in a mentor-protégé relationship as a protégé before assuming their first roles as presidents. More importantly, in the context of preparing future leaders for the presidency in the new millennium, more than 85 percent are now participating in either a formal or informal mentor-protégé relationship as a mentor" (p. 117).

A final area of consideration is to determine if the institution has a succession plan. More than ever, senior leaders are identifying potential emerging leaders and giving them a chance to understand and engage in change leadership experiences. Succession planning is generally equated with replacement planning, and the focus is on preparation, performance, and potential. Charan, Drotter, and Noel (2001) posit that "succession planning is perpetuating the enterprise by filling the pipeline with high-performing people to assure that every leadership level has an abundance of these performers to draw from, both now and in the future" (p. 167).

Conclusion

There are many leadership opportunities in the community college environment. Aspiring leaders have the responsibility to plan their own leadership preparation through engagement, planning, credentialing, and emulating throughout the entire process. It is clear that opportunities await those willing to be change leaders and accept the challenges of leadership in today's community colleges.

References

American Association of Community Colleges. *Competencies for Community College Leaders.* (Brochure). Washington, D.C.: American Association of Community Colleges, 2005.

Amey, M. J., and VanDerLinden, K. E. "Career Paths for Community College Leaders." Research Brief Leadership Series, no. 2, AACC-RB-02–2. Washington, D.C.: American Association of Community Colleges, 2002.

Boggs, G. R. "Leadership Context for the Twenty-First Century." In W. E. Piland and D. B. Wolf (eds.), *Help Wanted: Preparing Community College Leaders in a New Century.* New Directions for Community Colleges, no. 123, pp. 15–25. San Francisco: Jossey-Bass, 2003.

Charan, R., Drotter, S., and Noel, J. *The Leadership Pipeline: How to Build a Leadership Powered Company.* San Francisco: Jossey-Bass, 2001.

Community College Leadership Development Initiative. "Meeting New Leadership Challenges in the Community Colleges." Claremont Graduate University, Calif. ERIC Document Reproduction no. ED 447 888, 2000.

Duree, C. A. "The Challenges of the Community College Presidency in the New Millennium: Pathways, Preparation, Competencies and Leadership Programs Needed to Survive." Unpublished doctoral dissertation, Iowa State University, 2007.

Garza Mitchell, R. L., and Eddy, P. L. "In the Middle: Career Pathways of Midlevel Community College Leaders." *Community College Journal of Research and Practice,* 2008, *32*, 793–811.

Goleman, D. *Working with Emotional Intelligence.* New York: Bantam Dell, 1998.

Hull, J. R., and Kiem, M. C. "Nature and Status of Community College Leadership Development Programs." *Community College Journal of Research and Practice,* 2007, *31*, 689–702.

Jeandron, C. *Growing Your Own Leaders: Community Colleges Step Up.* Washington, D.C.: American Association of Community Colleges, 2006.

McDade, S. A. "Teacher-Pupil: The Changing Relationships of Mentors and Protégés." *Community College Journal of Research and Practice,* 2005, *29*, 759–781.

McFarlin, C. H., Crittenden, B. J., and Ebbers, L. H. "Background Factors Common Among Outstanding Community College Presidents." *Community College Review*, 1997, 27(3), 19–31.

Shults, C. "The Critical Impact of Impending Retirements on Community College Leadership." Research Brief Leadership Series, no. 1, AACC-RB-01–5. Washington, D.C.: American Association of Community Colleges, 2001.

Weisman, I., and Vaughan, G. *The Community College Presidency: 2006.* Washington, DC: American Association of Community Colleges, 2007.

LARRY EBBERS is university professor and professor of higher education at Iowa State University.

KITTY S. CONOVER is director emeritus of the Iowa Lakes Community College Center in Spencer, Iowa.

ANISHA SAMUELS is assistant director of the CLIC Program at Iowa State University.

A framework for understanding the human side of leadership, especially wounding and leadership struggles, is described with an emphasis on stories of community college presidents. Practical advice and recommendations are offered to better equip aspiring and practicing community college presidents for leadership challenges. A key message is that when a leader experiences a crisis, this stressful situation can be used as an opportunity to learn and grow.

Beyond the Headlines: Wounding and the Community College Presidency

Deborah L. Floyd, Pat Maslin-Ostrowski, Michael R. Hrabak

Media reports about budget deficits, bankruptcy and bailouts, unemployment, and the roller coaster that the nation's stock market and investments have become generate a constant bombardment of depressing news today. Across the nation, community colleges are experiencing daunting challenges that stem from economic and political uncertainties, compounded by turnover of leadership and expectations of doing much more with less. This context creates tremendous challenges for a community college president.

Yet, like community college presidents before them, contemporary leaders must prepare for an array of issues ranging from funding, faculty turnover, and fluctuating enrollment to demands from a board of trustees who may have little tolerance for errors by the president. The leadership challenges of diminishing resources are daunting but not entirely new; presidents before them have led colleges through tough times. In fact, George Vaughan's study (2000) of experienced community college presidents revealed valuable lessons learned amid times of crisis, including the importance of the president taking care of himself or herself. If leaders are to be successful, they must develop not only entrepreneurial agendas and strategic plans but strong support systems, as well as invest in personal and professional growth and development. This aspect of leadership, however, is often forgotten or neglected in the frantically paced, action-oriented world of administration. Yet presidents, like all leaders, will eventually find themselves experiencing a difficult situation, sometimes even a crisis. Leaders

NEW DIRECTIONS FOR COMMUNITY COLLEGES, no. 149, Spring 2010 © 2010 Wiley Periodicals, Inc.
Published online in Wiley InterScience (www.interscience.wiley.com) • DOI: 10.1002/cc.397

and crisis, and how to use such experiences for good, are the focus of this chapter.

A leadership crisis can be exaggerated and magnified through the media, particularly Internet sources. Even the most skilled president cannot be assured of any sense of privacy today, especially with the immediacy of technology through email, blogs, YouTube, Facebook, Twitter, and other commonly used mass-communication tools. A story that a reporter would have spent days researching in the past may now appear online within hours of receipt of a tip—only to be preempted by a blog posting or YouTube video. Every day events instantly balloon out of proportion to the level of a crisis, or an event is played out in real time with the advent of the "people's media," the Internet.

It takes a special person to face the complex and often personal challenges of leadership in a context of change. In this chapter, we describe a framework for understanding the human side of leadership during a crisis experience and offer practical recommendations to better equip aspiring and practicing community college presidents. An important message is that when a leader is experiencing a crisis, he or she may use this as an opportunity to learn and grow.

Background

The research in Vaughan's book *Balancing the Presidential Seesaw: Case Studies in Community College Leadership* (2000) served as a foundation for thinking about presidents and crisis. Vaughan reported the results of a survey and interviews he conducted with community college presidents who confronted difficult situations associated with votes of no confidence, termination, and resignation in the face of allegations or problematic working conditions; many of these presidents had also led through difficult economic times. The presidents Vaughan studied described the lessons they learned from their experiences; we address these lessons toward the end of this chapter.

To grasp the high stakes of leading a community college in today's environment, we reviewed the *Chronicle of Higher Education* for a five-year period, from 2003 to 2008. To limit the search and results, specific keywords were searched: "community college president," "fired," "no confidence," and "conflict." The *Chronicle* search yielded 24 hits (retrieved March 3, 2009). In contrast, a Google search yielded 9,550 hits using the same keywords (retrieved April 1, 2009). Many stories never make it to the *Chronicle*, remaining more of an internal affair, but this method was a starting point and served as a backdrop for stories of leaders in community colleges today.

It would have been preferable to conduct interviews with the community college leaders profiled in the *Chronicle*, but the purpose was simply to take the pulse of the presidency and certain crisis experiences. It is important to note that many conflicts, votes of no confidence, and firings do not make it to the national press and therefore were not identified in the *Chronicle*. In addition, when incidents do make the press, the story often becomes muddled. The examples gathered are of leaders who may have made some mistakes—or may have done nothing wrong but nonetheless found themselves in the middle of a crisis. The aim is to build on the public stories to develop better understanding of the inner crisis experience of community college leaders.

Framing Wounding and Leader Struggles

The role and responsibilities of a community college president can be overwhelming in the best of times, but especially during periods of turmoil and rapid change. Expectations for today's educational leaders are expanding as missions shift to reflect societal changes. For many, this change is occurring while resources are drastically reduced. Yet students, faculty, staff, and the community have hopes and dreams for their colleges that the leaders are expected to transform into reality. A wise leader recognizes the potential peril of holding on to traditional modes of operating in the face of new challenges. This means having to direct and redirect the organization, which often requires asking people to change their ways and rethink dearly held beliefs and values. People begin to push back and resist for their own reasons. This places the president in a position prime for crisis, the kind that may become personal. A leader may begin to wonder: Why am I here? Am I up to the challenges? Can I lead and be true to myself?

The research of Ackerman and Maslin-Ostrowski (2002, 2004) offers a simple framework for understanding the crisis experience of educational leaders. Their work is based on a series of interpretive phenomenological studies that are guided by two essential questions: "First, how does a reasonable, well-intentioned leader preserve a healthy sense of self when that self is challenged or even wounded? Second, what perspective on the leader's work can enhance understanding of the challenges and produce a mind-set that leaves the leader open to learn and grow from such experiences?" (2004, p. 310). Although their research focused on school leaders, it has been identified as relevant to higher education, including community college executives, and in particular the presidency (Floyd and Casey, 2004).

One of the core understandings of Ackerman and Maslin-Ostrowski's research states that crises and dilemmas are inevitably part of leadership. A leader inhabits the realm of action and, as a change agent, is engaged in risky work. If a leader is going to enter the messy and complex world of educational organizations and not sit on the sidelines, then eventually he or she will become enmeshed in some kind of crisis experience. Leader stories tell of experiences that "wound them," the kind of experience where a leader's identity or integrity is called into question (2002, p. 17).

Another core understanding that they write about is a need for leaders to be keenly tuned in to the inner work of leadership. The intrapersonal and interpersonal sides of leadership, they contend, are just as important as the traditional sides of leadership that focus on strategy, skills, and competencies. Cultivating emotional awareness, making time for reflection, and

New Directions for Community Colleges • DOI: 10.1002/cc

engaging in collegial inquiry are ways to cope with the demands and allow leaders to be whole and fulfill their mandate to lead.

Ackerman and Maslin-Ostrowski describe how leaders navigate the territory of leadership, a life that is characterized by vulnerability, power, isolation, and fear. These four givens (and they acknowledge there are others) are said to be endemic conditions that are particularly heightened during times of crisis.

Drawing on the stories found in the *Chronicle*, we identified contexts for crisis scenarios that could permit insight as to how a leader might experience these difficult conditions. Although the examples represent huge professional and personal challenges to community college presidents, what becomes a wounding experience for one individual may not be the same for another. In the examples given, the institutions and individual identities are disguised, identifying details are omitted, and quotes are paraphrased to support the utmost confidentiality.

Vulnerability

Ackerman and Maslin-Ostrowski posit that leaders are vulnerable to having their integrity and identity challenged—in other words, to being wounded. The tension of a leader living up to role expectations contributes to a leader's vulnerability. Leaders often act as if they are supposed to be invulnerable, yet Ackerman and Maslin-Ostrowski found that it is often through vulnerability that a leader looks inward and is then able to learn and develop.

Leaders are change agents, which puts them in the center of conflict, and when the conflict plays out in the press they become especially vulnerable to being misunderstood and hurt. As a college controversy unfolds, particularly amid wide media coverage, the president may feel the pressure of being the point person and lightning rod for the conflict. This can become painful for presidents who discover that what is being communicated in the public discourse does not fit with who they believe they are as a leader.

To illustrate, a popular president of a rural community college was tapped to serve as president of the state's largest community college in a metropolitan area. Well liked by students and professors, the president was demoted to faculty in a surprise move by the board. This action was taken following the release of a report by an investigator hired by the state chancellor regarding questionable college contracts and appointments. Critics accused the president of undermining the state chancellor and state board, while the governor and others criticized the board for their lack of due process in the president's ouster. The crisis unfolded in the public arena, which likely exacerbated the loss of control the president felt and led to feelings of self-doubt. The president, caught in the middle, spoke of wanting a chance to tell her side of the story and was determined to be vindicated. Without a doubt, everyday crises occur frequently without such fanfare, yet this still may lead to feelings of vulnerability, the kind where a leader begins to doubt himself or herself.

Power

As noted by Ackerman and Maslin-Ostrowski, when a leader is in a crisis there is usually loss of control and new awareness of the ambiguities of power. A leader may be confronted by the elusive nature of power despite the position. The focus of this study is the community college president, clearly a high-level position with authority, yet power is not sufficient for all to control the situation or even to maintain their job. In fact, community college boards may choose to hold the president accountable even if the president is the person who uncovered improprieties; a leader's position does not come with all the power that many imagine it holds.

To illustrate this dilemma: a community college president was fired by a board following a football scandal where two former coaches were indicted for federal charges that included fraud, theft, and embezzlement. Only a few months earlier the board had given the president a letter of commendation for bringing the problem to the forefront but subsequently decided to fire him, stating the policy that the board holds the president accountable if unlawful practices occurred. According to the president, the unlawful practices had never been allowed but were concealed by the athletic department, and when he discovered what was happening he immediately took action to correct it. Despite doing what he believed to be the right thing by "blowing the whistle" on the coaches' improprieties, ultimately the president's power was diminished and he lost his job.

Isolation

Contrary to the emphasis today on collaboration and cooperation, Ackerman and Maslin-Ostrowski report that leaders still tend to feel alone and isolated, which intensifies during a crisis. Leaders experience a unique type of isolation in that they spend their days (and many evenings and weekends), with people in connection to their institution, yet because of matters of confidentiality, decision making, and other responsibilities, they must erect boundaries at work and in the surrounding community. Some leaders also create boundaries between their inner life of reflection and outer life of action.

An ultimate form of isolation comes when a community college leader is placed on paid leave and an investigation is launched, thereby forcing the leader into isolation. This painful act can occur whether a president is guilty of any wrongdoing or not. For instance, a community college president with more than eight years' experience was placed on paid leave for three months pending the outcome of an investigation of spending practices. From the president's perspective, the action was based on a false report and was politically motivated by the county executive, who appointed a majority of the board. The president proclaimed her innocence, citing the board for retaliating against her refusal to make certain personnel decisions. This is an extreme example, but isolation can occur daily for a president even when surrounded by supportive faculty, staff, and students. In this case, the college faculty supported the president and indeed asked the board to reinstate her. During such times of crisis, presidents are painfully reminded how lonely they remain at the top.

Fear

According to Ackerman and Maslin-Ostrowski, fear is inherent in a leader's life. Fears of all sorts show up: of public failure, of being judged, of falling short of expectations. For some, there is the fear of changing, or the fear of not changing. Though not reported in the media as such, presidents who follow long-serving leaders may fear not being fully accepted or not living up to expectations. As a record number of community college presidents retire and new people transition into the positions, these fears may be actualized. Although the fears of presidents are often hidden from public view, perhaps from a cultural bias toward heroic leaders who are invincible, they are not immune to such emotions.

Confronting, not dismissing, fear has the potential to lead to positive outcomes. A president, for example, was embroiled in conflict with two members of the board of trustees and resisted the board's micromanagement of college operations, yet this president left without being fired or experiencing a no-confidence vote, and with limited media attention. Perhaps this president was able to face any fears about being perceived a failure for walking away from the office. Instead, the president left on independent terms for a university administrative position. The president talked about his need to take stock of the kind of leader he was and wondered if he was leading in the way he wanted; or was he becoming a distraction? This demonstrates how a crisis experience can become an opening to reflect and learn about oneself.

Surviving the Human Hazards of Leading Change

As Vaughan (2000) asserts, the job of a community college president comes with great exhilaration and, many times, difficult challenges that can decimate one personally, professionally, and emotionally. Dubois notes that "the expectations are increasing. The need to . . . respond to unmet community needs is greater and greater and greater" (cited in Fain, 2006, p. A28). He adds that a president needs support to survive. Recognizing the potential human hazards of leading change, we propose some commonsense recommendations that may be a beginning point of guidance for leaders to cope and learn while experiencing times of crisis. Leaders sometimes need a jolt, or at other times merely a gentle reminder or refresher, to remain on their intended path and mission. We hope these recommendations will constitute a revival of familiar themes that most know but might have forgotten.

Leader as Learner

- Be open to using a crisis experience as a learning opportunity.
- Presidents no longer have the luxury of a grace period, so build a network of support—people to learn from and with—upon entry.
- Be clear and confident about personal values and beliefs. Establish professional boundaries.
- Crisis and even loss of a job can help clarify and reclaim one's career identity.
- Listen and learn. Alternatively, to borrow from W. E. B. Dubois, "lead with your ears" (cited in Fain, 2006).
- Always have an exit plan and the willingness to reframe, to be able to leave on independent terms and in a graceful fashion.

Power for Good

- Know the expectations before accepting a job, and know that expectations can change with the wind as political power shifts.
- Set ego aside, and realize that a president is a placeholder in a position of power, and thus the focus of praise during good times and criticism during difficult times.
- Create a work culture where power is shared and where all members—including the president—are able to grow and develop.

Emotional Maturity

- Emotions are part of leading and are to be embraced.
- Face fear with openness and respect, not arrogance.
- Be adaptable and consider multiple perspectives.
- Use emotion for good, never for harm.
- Pay attention to physical well-being and emotional health.

Stay Connected

- Have a good friend, and be a good friend.
- Develop a personal network of sitting presidents and former presidents.
- Find a mentor. Be a mentor.
- Create local and external webs of trusted colleagues.
- Learn how to use fast-paced communication technologies and media to enhance interpersonal connections.
- Establish equilibrium between life at work and home. The presidency is just a job.
- Carve out time to stop, think, and reflect regularly.
- Turn to spirituality.

A Leader in Times of Challenge and Change

The headline is that there are steps presidents can take toward practicing leadership in a way that will sustain them during a crisis experience. This chapter has chronicled the experience of community college presidents who found themselves in difficult circumstances, many of which were outside their control, and sometimes a leader in this position may discover he or she does not have the relationships, connections, self-awareness, or just plain luck to survive, let alone learn from the crisis. To serve as a community college president, one of the most demanding and taxing jobs in higher education, makes one vulnerable. Yet a wounding experience, the kind where a leader's integrity and identity are questioned, can become "a catalyst for a leader to grow" (Ackerman and Maslin-Ostrowski, 2002, p. 12). The hope is that leaders become better equipped to cope and eventually transform a crisis into good. Presidents and the institutions they serve are urged to develop strong support systems and a collegial work environment, to allow leaders to hold onto the passion that brought them to the profession in the beginning, and to thrive in times of challenge and change.

References

Ackerman, R. H., and Maslin-Ostrowski, P. *The Wounded Leader: How Real Leadership Emerges in Times of Crisis.* San Francisco: Jossey Bass, 2002.

Ackerman, R. H., and Maslin-Ostrowski, P. "The Wounded Leader and Emotional Learning in the Schoolhouse." *School Leadership and Management,* 2004, 24(3), 309–326.

Fain, P. "Crisis of Confidence." *Chronicle of Higher Education,* June 23, 2006. Retrieved Mar. 2, 2009, from http://chronicle.com/weekly/v52/i42/42a02801.htm.

Floyd, D. L., and Casey, D. "Review of *The Wounded Leader: How Real Leadership Emerges in Times of Crisis.*" *Community College Journal of Research and Practice,* 2004, 28(2), 165–166.

Vaughan, G. B. *Balancing the Presidential Seesaw: Case Studies in Community College Leadership.* Washington, D.C.: Community College Press, 2000.

DEBORAH L. FLOYD *is a professor and doctoral coordinator of higher education leadership at Florida Atlantic University and a former community college president, vice president, and dean of students.*

PAT MASLIN-OSTROWSKI *is a professor of school leadership at Florida Atlantic University whose work centers on the social-emotional dimensions of leadership and the quest for more effective policy and practice to support leader learning.*

MICHAEL R. HRABAK *is a doctoral student at Florida Atlantic University specializing in the study of community college curriculum and leadership.*

9

*Change leadership and leadership development are criti-
cally important to the continuing success of public community colleges everywhere. Transactional and
transformational leadership, the more traditional models,
are no longer adequate to meet the pressing financial and
operational challenges in two-year institutions. Current
and aspiring leaders must understand the culture of
change that permeates community college campuses and
embrace the opportunities inherent in that culture.*

Epilogue: Change Leadership and Leadership Development

Robert C. Cloud

Current community college change leadership evolved from traditional public school bureaucratic models that emphasized control and oversight. In
fact, many two-year colleges developed as an upward extension of local public schools (Cohen and Brawer, 2003). The school board approved the college budget and governed college operations, and the superintendent often
served as the college president. Public school teachers taught college classes
part-time in school facilities after regular school hours. As a rule, faculty
members were not invited to participate in the management and leadership
of the college. Teachers taught students, and administrators made the decisions. Having served as public school administrators before moving into
two-year college administration, many presidents projected a paternalistic
attitude toward teachers (Cohen and Brawer). There was little or no commitment to the principles of shared governance, participative management,
and collaborative decision making that are mainstays of current change leadership. The centralized public school model was adequate so long as colleges were small, the curriculum was narrow, and operations remained
relatively simple.

From their inception in the early twentieth century until the 1960s,
most two-year institutions were known as junior colleges (Cohen and
Brawer, 2003). During the late 1960s, however, many junior colleges
adopted comprehensive mission statements, expanded their curricula, and
negotiated partnerships with various constituencies (Cohen and Brawer).
Consequently, the term "community college" was coined to describe these

NEW DIRECTIONS FOR COMMUNITY COLLEGES, no. 149, Spring 2010 © 2010 Wiley Periodicals, Inc.
Published online in Wiley InterScience (www.interscience.wiley.com) • DOI: 10.1002/cc.398

more complex, community-based colleges. Autocratic administrators were ill equipped to lead such comprehensive institutions, and the all-powerful presidents of the past retired or were replaced (Cohen and Brawer).

Community college leadership has since evolved into a dynamic process with a host of participants. Gone are the days when administrators act unilaterally and arbitrarily on college issues. Although the president retains the final authority to carry out assigned duties, prudent leaders insist on broad-based participation in the leadership process, for obvious reasons. Nationwide, the current trend is toward increased involvement and shared responsibility in college change leadership (Cloud and Kater, 2008).

Change Leadership

In Chapter One, Desna Wallin defines change leadership as a four-part process that *anticipates* change, *analyzes* the internal and external environments, *acts* on the basis of appropriate and timely data and the strengths of team members, and *affirms* institutional actions with the goal of continuous organizational improvement. In its finest form, change leadership is a moral act, based on ethical actions, that serves the long-term interests of the college and its constituencies. Change leadership is more complex than either transactional or transformational leadership. The former focuses primarily on maintenance and management of the status quo with incremental changes as needed; the latter facilitates systemic change through the leader's articulated vision and a motivated workforce (Roueche, Baker, and Rose, 1989). Change leadership, by contrast, facilitates changes in both employees and the organization. Community college change leaders create a "culture of change" where faculty and staff are encouraged to brainstorm current and anticipated issues and recommend changes. Change leaders seek out employees with leadership potential and prepare them for future leadership roles through a formal succession plan, thus ensuring stability and continuity in the college administration (Mathis and Jackson, 2009). They also develop leadership centers that analyze anticipated threats and opportunities and prepare college action plans accordingly. Change leaders think and act outside the box when appropriate and motivate others to do the same.

Leadership Development

Leadership development is a formal and informal process that is intended to maximize institutional and individual effectiveness. There are at least three components in the leadership development process: (1) university-based academic credit programs that enhance knowledge, skills, and competencies and that often lead to a master's or doctoral degree; (2) in-service or developmental programs for practicing leaders sponsored by professional organizations, governmental agencies, or higher education institutions; and (3) informal and lifelong learning strategies that enable leaders at all levels to increase their knowledge of management and leadership processes and improve performance. These informal strategies may include professional reading, personal reflection, travel, writing for publication, and active involvement in professional organizations.

This volume reviews the range of leadership development opportunities available to community college professionals, from partnerships to the community college baccalaureate initiative to reflective learning strategies. Two exemplary doctoral leadership programs are profiled in Chapters Four and Six. Chapter Seven highlights local college efforts to "grow your own" leaders through various developmental activities for motivated middle managers. In Chapter Eight, the authors acknowledge that community college change leaders (agents) work in a risky environment and suggest that presidents consider the inevitable crises and personal attacks that wound them and their families as opportunities to grow personally and professionally—an interesting perspective indeed.

Necessary Personal Qualities of Change Leaders

Implementing the four components of change leadership in public community colleges is difficult and can be hazardous to the health and career of an administrative leader. In addition to the required academic credentials, professional experience, and administrative skills, successful leaders have certain personal qualities that are essential in fostering peaceful and productive change.

First, successful change leaders listen more than they talk or act.

Second, prudent leaders do not view themselves as "the boss" with the right to coerce subordinates or force institutional changes without appropriate dialog and planning. They consider themselves to be "first among equals" and invite others to join in a continuing effort to improve the college (Birnbaum, 1988). Effective change leaders understand that they lead with the consent of the led (Greenleaf, 1991). Consequently, they encourage cooperation and inclusion and make it clear that all administrative actions are accountable to stakeholders.

Third, successful change leaders are motivated to serve before they aspire to lead. As "servant leaders," they are committed to helping students and colleagues become wiser, healthier, more productive, and more independent because of their experiences at the college (Greenleaf, 1991). Ideally, change leaders view their positional authority as significant only as a means to the primary end of serving students, the community, and the profession.

Fourth, change leaders articulate a vision for their college and then persuade colleagues and supporters to help with its implementation. Because coercion invariably alienates those subjected to it, leaders do not coerce; their goal is cooperation, not control (Cohen and Brawer, 2003).

Fifth, as documented in Chapter Three of this volume, effective leaders have a high degree of emotional intelligence, meaning they are highly motivated, self-disciplined, empathic, and caring individuals (Goleman, 2004). Blessed with superior interpersonal skills, leaders with emotional intelligence treat others with respect and empower subordinates to carry out duties expeditiously and compassionately. Secure in themselves and confident in their purpose, change leaders question existing policies and practices and encourage colleagues to develop new and innovative ways to increase institutional effectiveness. Though advocating for improvement of college practices, emotionally intelligent leaders respect the institution's heritage and are as careful as possible not to offend alumni, faculty, and staff who cherish its related traditions.

Sixth and finally, change leaders are authentic individuals who eschew pretense. They are comfortable with themselves and open with others. Even though they respect power, they are not intimidated by it. Authentic leaders confront the phony when necessary. Gentle and kind by nature, authentic leaders treat everyone with respect—the powerful and the powerless, rich and poor alike (Starratt, 2004). Consequently, authentic change leaders are trusted and respected by their peers, who are then more likely to support leadership proposals for necessary changes in the college.

College leaders who do not possess all or most of these qualities will likely be very lonely once they are terminated, resign, or retire.

Necessary Competencies for Change Leaders

In addition to required personal qualities, community college change leaders must possess specific professional competencies if they are to lead responsibly and effectively. In recognition of that fact, the W. K. Kellogg Foundation awarded the American Association of Community Colleges (AACC) a grant titled Leading Forward to address the national need for community college leaders. AACC began the Leading Forward initiative in 2003 by hosting a series of four daylong leadership summits with different constituent groups. The purpose of the summits was to develop consensus around the key competencies and skills needed by two-year college leaders and determine how to best develop and support leaders. Experts in community college leadership from AACC affiliate councils, colleges in underserved areas, and university graduate programs convened in Washington, D.C., between November 2003 and March 2004. A total of 168 higher education professionals participated in the four summits. On April 9, 2005, the AACC board of directors approved the final *Leading Forward* document and encouraged college leaders to use six competencies in the report as standards for performance assessment:

1. **Organizational strategy.** An effective community college leader improves the quality of the institution, protects the long-term health of

the organization, promotes the success of all students, and sustains the college mission.

2. **Resource management.** An effective community college leader equitably and ethically sustains people and processes as well as institutional assets to fulfill the mission, vision, and goals of the college.

3. **Communication.** An effective community college leader uses clear communication skills to engage in honest, open dialogue at all levels of the college and its surrounding community, to promote the success of all students, and to sustain the college mission.

4. **Collaboration.** An effective community college leader develops and maintains cooperative, mutually beneficial, and ethical relationships that nurture diversity and sustain the college mission. Change leaders, in particular, must be adept at conflict resolution and consensus building.

5. **Community college advocacy.** An effective community college leader understands, commits to, and advocates for the mission, vision, and goals of the college.

6. **Professionalism.** An effective community college leader works ethically to set high standards for self and others, continuously improve self and surroundings, demonstrate accountability to and for the institution, and ensure the long-term viability of the college and community.

> [AACC, Competencies for Community College Leaders,
> 2005, adapted]

Community college change leaders should embrace the personal qualities and professional competencies discussed in this chapter. They will have need of these talents as they grapple with current and predicted issues, many of which defy solution.

Issues Facing Change Leaders

A public community college is a microcosm of the society that funds it. Consequently, change leaders are confronted with a range of economic, social, political, and operational issues that complicate the leadership process. These examples reflect that range:

- Governing boards must be educated about the change leadership process through local, state, and national initiatives.
- Safety and security are primary concerns on all community college campuses. For obvious reasons, change leaders must make this issue a top priority.
- Community college enrollments, currently experiencing double-digit increases, will continue to escalate nationwide (N. G. Kent, AACC vice president for communications, personal conversation, Oct 13, 2009). A growing number of students will require remediation.

- Local taxpayer resistance is a reality in many college districts.
- Special interest groups, including taxpayers' associations and teachers' unions, will continue supporting candidates in governing board elections, creating potentially volatile situations for change leaders.
- The number of part-time teachers, now at approximately 66 percent of the total faculty workforce, will continue to increase, raising legitimate concerns about instructional quality and faculty participation in governance (Levin, Kater, and Wagoner, 2006).
- Community college faculty, already the most unionized of all faculties in postsecondary education, will press for better compensation and meaningful participation in administration and governance (Cohen and Brawer, 2003).
- College partnerships with public and private agencies will increase as pressures mount to do more with less.
- K–16 initiatives will require closer collaboration among the principals than ever before.
- Proprietary institutions will recruit more students away from community colleges with the promise of accelerated degree plans, job-specific training, and guaranteed placement at graduation.
- Single-issue and rogue board members will not be helpful to change leaders seeking necessary changes in the college.
- Finally, public community colleges exist in a highly litigious society. Consequently, change leaders must deal with the added threat of litigation as they implement needed, but controversial, changes in college policies and practices (Cloud, 2004).

In summary, community college change leaders serve in a dynamic environment that is no place for the timid or faint-hearted. In addition to the previously suggested qualities and competencies, a thick hide and a sense of humor will be helpful to leaders as they carry out assigned duties.

References

American Association of Community Colleges (AACC). *Competencies for Community College Leaders*. Washington, D.C.: AACC, 2005.

Birnbaum, R. *How Colleges Work: The Cybernetics of Academic Organization and Leadership*. San Francisco: Jossey-Bass, 1988.

Cloud, R. C. (ed.). *Legal Issues in the Community College*. San Francisco: Jossey-Bass, 2004.

Cloud, R. C., and Kater, S. T. (eds.). *Governance in the Community College*. San Francisco: Jossey-Bass, 2008.

Cohen, A. M., and Brawer, F. B. *The American Community College* (4th ed.). San Francisco: Jossey-Bass, 2003.

Goleman, D. "What Makes a Leader?" *Harvard Business Review*, 2004, 82(1), 82–96.

Greenleaf, R. K. *The Servant as Leader*. Cambridge, Mass.: Center for Applied Studies, 1991.

Levin, J. S., Kater, S. T., and Wagoner, R. L. *Community College Faculty: At Work in the New Economy*. New York: Palgrave Macmillan, 2006.

Mathis, R. L., and Jackson, J. H. *Human Resource Management: Essential Perspectives.* Mason, Ohio: South-Western College Learning, 2009.

Roueche, J. E., Baker, G. A., and Rose, R. R. *Shared Vision: Transformational Leadership in American Community Colleges.* Washington, D.C.: American Association of Community Colleges, 1989.

Starratt, R. J. *Ethical Leadership.* San Francisco: Jossey-Bass, 2004.

ROBERT C. CLOUD is professor of higher education at Baylor University.

INDEX